Wisdom
On
Stepparenting

How to Succeed
Where Others Fail

Diana Weiss-Wisdom, Ph.D.

ISBN-10: 1467966002
ISBN-13: 9781467966009
Library of Congress Control Number: 2012906635
CreateSpace, North Charleston, South Carolina

Wisdom on Stepparenting

Diana Weiss-Wisdom, PhD

"Stepparenting can be as rewarding as it is challenging. *Wisdom on Stepparenting: How to Succeed Where Others Fail* will skillfully guide you through mishaps and setbacks as you build a bridge toward compassion and heartfelt connection."

—Judy Ford, LCSW, author of *Wonderful Ways to Love a Child, Wonderful Ways to Be a Stepparent,* and *Everyday Love Day: The Delicate Art of Caring for Each Other.*

"As a Certified California Family Law Specialist for the last 38 years I have seen the destruction of new relationships because couples do not have the knowledge, tools or insight to address the blending of step families. The divorce rate for second marriages is higher than first marriages. This book provides excellent psychological knowledge, Wise insights and practical interactive tools to arm yourself with so that you and your family do not become part of those statistics."

—Beatrice L. Snider, attorney, Certified Family Law Specialist San Diego, California.

"This book combines helpful, realistic examples and wise advice to help the reader understand and cope with the challenges of being in a stepfamily. A prescription for making marital and stepfamily complexity work—read this."

—Carl Pickhardt, PhD, author of
Surviving Your Child's Adolescence.

"Diana writes from a place of real life experience in which she shares a wealth of practical and loving wisdom balanced with sensitivity for each step member which fosters healthy relating and tremendous hope in helping stepfamilies to be happier and more connected with one another."

—Tami Chelew, MFT, Marriage Educator

"This book provides a wonderful roadmap through stepfamily life. Easy to read and touching on all the right notes, a must read for all couples in remarried life with kids!"

—Susan Davis-Swanson, PhD, LCSW and
Director of The StepFamily Center.

"This gem of a book reveals how stepparenting, in spite of the pitfalls can be done well and be immensely rewarding for the whole family."

—Richard Levak, Ph.D., Licensed Psychologist and
Personality Expert.

"WE ARE THE LEAVES OF ONE BRANCH,
THE DROPS OF ONE SEA, THE FLOWERS OF ONE GARDEN."
—*Jean-Baptiste Henri Lacordaire*

Dedication

TO MY HUSBAND GABRIEL FOR HIS UNENDING LOVE, PATIENCE, AND INSPIRATION

Acknowledgements

Thank you to Joe Tash, Anne Geiberger, and Shannon Moore for their expert editing assistance.

Many thanks to Lorine Wright for giving me the opportunity to write for the San Diego Rancho Coast News Group; writing my biweekly column for your newspaper has helped me develop the discipline and confidence to write this book.

Thank you to Katherine Quinn, Rachel Goldenhar, Claudia Dunaway, Janie De Celles, Laura Struhl, Marlene Maheu, Donna Genett, Barbara and Howard Milstein, Linda Rock, Richard Levak, Beth and Sean Hogan, Jeff Jones, Katherine De Bruin, Jessica Buss, and Rebecca Jorgensen for their ongoing feedback, encouragement, and support. Thank you to Drs. Sue Johnson, John Gottman, Harville Hendrix, Shelly Gable, and Barbara Fredrickson for their valuable research and guidance on creating loving relationships.

A special thank you to my mother and stepfather for all their support during my adjustment to stepfamily life. Thank you to my father-in-law Irv, for his love and always believing in me. Thank you to my sister for her friendship and support. Thank you to my brother, sister-in-law, Uncle, and Aunt for being such great role models for how to raise a loving family. Thank you Dani, Julia, Kevin, Marc *and Lauren, Rachel, and Ryan, Noah, Lily, Ella, and Charlotte for all of the joy that you bring to our lives. Lastly, but not least, thank you to my stepdaughters for their friendship, perseverance and love - without them, I would not have been inspired to write this book.*

Table of Contents

Introduction

Some people say that adults don't fully mature until they have children, because parenthood requires a greater level of responsibility and commitment. Being a stepparent is a similar rite of passage on the road to character development and social evolution, with its own unique twists. In the best scenarios, stepparents can promote healing and growth in their new families. And gradually, we can all help to transform the world into a more peaceful and loving place.

Someone recently asked me, "So what's it like, being a stepmother?" Truthfully, my answer may differ depending on when the question is asked. But, generally speaking, being a stepmother has been a uniquely challenging and rewarding experience. There have been so many lessons to learn along the way, and these lessons have become helpful to my growth as a person.

Just as the human species is one human family, my stepchildren are, in a spiritual sense, my very own children. But this doesn't mean that the relationships we have need to be a certain way, or that my stepdaughters needed a stepparent. In our family's case, they really didn't. They have two involved, loving parents already. It means that by marrying their father, I have committed myself to being a constant in my stepdaughters' lives. And with all my heart, I want my contribution to their lives to be a positive one.

For most of us stepparents, our role is a supporting one. The extent of involvement for each person depends on a multitude of factors, including basic chemistry. But we do get to decide how we want to behave and the attitude that we bring to the family.

Just like many of you, I had no idea how challenging it is to be a stepparent until I walked in those shoes myself. It is not unusual for stepparents to feel like they've taken on more than they expected. Sometimes, this can be in terms of added responsibilities or having to cope with one's own reactions to the new family.

I've been a student of human behavior since I was a little girl. Over the years, I watched my own family morph into a stepfamily. I have a stepfather, heard about my grandmother's wicked stepmother, became a licensed clinical psychologist, studied stepfamilies, have worked with stepfamilies in my practice, continue to write an advice column on marriage and stepfamilies for the local newspaper (since 2004), and have been a stepmother for ten years.

I started writing this book after I'd been married for a couple of years, because it helped me to sort out my own thoughts. Delving into my own experiences and those of my clients, I tried to mine for precious metal. I looked for nuggets of gold in the mix of soil and debris. Then I started interviewing stepmothers, stepfathers, and stepchildren, along with a few biological parents for good measure.

Woven throughout this book are strategies (proven to work through scientific research) tailored for stepparents on how to build positive relationships and how to live a healthy, happy life in a stepfamily. The names of the people in the stories have of course been changed, as have key details of the stories, to protect the privacy of those concerned.

Most of us get married because we fall in love and want to spend our lives with that special person. Initially, we often minimize the challenges that come with marrying someone with children from a prior relationship. Statistically, when there are children from a previous union in the mix, the chances for a successful relationship are lower than for first marriages.

Bottom line: Stepparents can have a significant role in cultivating a well-adjusted stepfamily. Resiliency skills and keeping certain feelings and perspectives in check can help you go the distance. This book is focused on the kind of mindset and behaviors that are conducive to success. These include making your marriage a priority, having reasonable expectations, personal strength, and commitment. I've distilled and presented specific practices and attitudes that have been proven to help people with relationships, resiliency, and happiness. These techniques are offered throughout this book, specifically tailored to the stepparent and stepfamily experience.

In today's world, people are talking more and more about the need for the human race to learn to get along and cooperate with one another in order for our species to survive. Stepfamilies are now outnumbering traditional nuclear families. In a way, stepfamilies are like a microcosm of our larger society and its competing need for resources and territorial concerns. If we are good role models and team players, our children learn from watching us. Children can then take what they learn about relationships, diversity, compassion, and resiliency in their stepfamilies out into the world. What do we want to teach them?

This book is intended to offer realistic hope and guidance on navigating the stepparenting trail in a way that promotes the wellbeing of you and your new family. I hope that it will be helpful to you on your own individual journey as well.

Sincerely,

Diana Weiss-Wisdom

Chapter One

Stepfamily 101

As human beings, we long for belonging. We form families and tribes because that's how we are wired to thrive. As stepparents, we join a pre-existing family, which then creates adjustments for each member. Depending on the chemistry and situation, some stepparents are more welcomed than others. Some may have the experience of never being fully accepted. There are many reasons why some family members may not fully embrace a stepparent. To some degree the family members' feelings make sense; their feelings have some basis in their particular reality that cause them to feel and behave the way they do. But for a stepparent, who must endure the full or partial rejection of their partner's child, it is especially important to make use of the tools in this book. You can still have a great marriage no matter how receptive the other people in the family are to you. Adopting a realistic and positive perspective backed with commitment and practical tools can enhance your chances of creating healthy, loving relationships in your stepfamily.

This chapter is a short primer on what a stepfamily or blended family is. Feel free to skip ahead. The simplest kind of stepfamily is one in which one member of the couple has a child or children from a previous relationship. The member of the couple who is not the biological parent of the child is then called the "stepmother"

1

or "stepfather." In a blended stepfamily, both adults in the couple have children from a prior relationship, or they may have additional children together. The children that each member of the couple brings to the marriage then become stepbrothers and stepsisters. If the couple then has a child together, that child is a half sister or half brother to the children that came from previous relationships.

The terms "stepfamily" and "blended family" are often used interchangeably. Some people think that "blended family" is a misleading label because it can create unrealistic expectations—sometimes stepfamilies don't blend very well if at all. Other times, they can bond just as well as biological families. With different personalities, situations, and interpersonal dynamics, just as in the traditional, nuclear family, every family is different. Each has its own unique strengths and challenges.

Having said that, there are certain trials and tribulations specific to stepfamilies in particular; some of these are addressed in this book—with a special emphasis on the role of stepparents in these dynamics. The main focus here is to help stepparents in their understanding and perspective when it comes to being a thriving and active member of a stepfamily. Here you will find tools and perspectives for coping, thriving, and contributing to your family in your own best way.

Even though stepfamilies are the new norm, roles and responsibilities of stepparents continue to be fuzzy. When children don't know what to expect in their relationships with stepparents or stepsiblings, it can be confusing. This lack of clarity and established social norms can cause frequent conflicts between parents and couples in regard to how relationships and households are managed.

Stepfamilies can encompass a number of configurations:
- Biological fathers with children, remarried, while ex-wife remains single
- Biological mothers with children, remarried, while ex-husband remains single
- Biological fathers and mothers who have both remarried

- Remarriages where both spouses bring children from a previous marriage so the children have stepsiblings
- Remarriages with stepchildren in which the newly married couple has a baby of their own
- Custody ranging from 100 percent to one person, to an 80–20 or 50–50 split
- Remarriages of widows or widowers with children
- One of the biological parents rarely, if ever, seeing the children for any number of reasons (e.g., incarceration, chronic mental illness)
- Stepparent adopting a child when neither parent is available or fit
- Stepfamilies that begin when all the children are adults
- Stepfamilies that begin with children under ten years old
- Stepfamilies with teenagers
- Stepfamilies with agreeable ex-spouses
- Stepfamilies with a lot of conflict or hostility remaining between biological parents

Naturally, each of these family combinations comes with different challenges and issues. By no means are most of these different types of stepfamilies specifically addressed in this book. Hopefully, the ideas presented here can be applied to a wide range of situations.

Over the years, as individual relationships grow, each does so in its own way—even within a stepfamily. Some family members are more open than others. Some children never get over a divorce, while others in the same family may appreciate how their parents are thriving in their new marriage. Sometimes stepchildren who resist accepting stepparents eventually see their stepparents as bonus parents. Children who have experienced the losses and changes inherent in divorce are vulnerable to feeling threatened or jealous of their stepparents. Those children may fear losing attention or love from a parent whom they already don't see often enough. When children are open to their stepparents, it is a huge gift and should be treated as such. Other times, stepparents need to walk on eggshells while divorce injuries heal. It can sometimes take a long time for the relationship to be less hindered by random pieces of floating or submerged driftwood that create blockages in the coursing river of human connection. Several chapters in this book focus on ways to navigate the unique challenges of creating and maintaining as positive of a relationship as possible with your stepchildren.

Chapter Two

It's Complicated

"A human being is part of the whole, called by us "universe,"
a part limited in time and space. He experiences himself, his thoughts
and feelings as something separated from the rest – a kind of optical
delusion of his consciousness."
—ALBERT EINSTEIN

Life had tossed Angela some rough curveballs. When her parents divorced, she was only five years old; she never saw her father again. Her mother had to support her two children and never remarried. Angela and her little sister were latchkey children. Angela was in charge most of the time; she made peanut butter and jelly sandwiches to fill their empty tummies.

Angela started hanging out with boys when she was fifteen years old. She was starved for attention and was drawn to "bad boys" who didn't treat her very well. They were delinquent types who got in frequent fistfights with other boys. As Angela got older, her boyfriends started pushing her around. By high school, her relationships were so rough and destructive that she barely made it through high school. She didn't have many friends, and after school, there weren't any adults around. She preferred the company of boys that didn't treat her well to being alone.

Angela married Sam when she was twenty years old. Sam was better than any man she had ever met. He was dependable, and he wanted her badly. It felt so good to be wanted like that. Once they married, Sam became even more possessive; when he didn't get his way, he yelled and bullied Angela until he did. Sam came from an abusive home where there was a lot of yelling and physical violence. He was proud that he never touched Angela or the kids in anger. But over time, the emotional roller coaster became too much, and when Angela and Sam divorced, the kids were actually relieved.

Two years after the divorce was final, Angela met Louis, a hardworking, happy-go-lucky kind of a guy. He came from a good family with a mom and a dad, a younger sister, a dog, a cat, and a swimming pool. Relatively speaking, he hadn't had much hardship in his life. He saw the world through rose-colored glasses, seeing the best in people without even trying. He loved to make Angela laugh. He would watch her serious face crinkle into a playful smile; his genuine belly laugh of delight that followed was contagious. Angela's corresponding laughter made his heart sing.

When Louis was with Angela, he felt comfortable and as if he were "home," no matter where they were. That's how he knew that she was the one for him. Their relationship seemed effortless as they fell in love with each other. As Louis had never been married, he was quite idealistic about becoming a husband and stepfather.

During Louis and Angela's courtship, they enjoyed each other intensely, and focused mainly on their one-on-one connection. Angela kept the children and her ex-husband out of it. She especially wanted to make sure that the relationship was working well before she introduced him to her children.

One day when they were away for a romantic weekend, Louis told Angela that he had never felt for a woman the way he did for her. He wanted to meet her children and move forward with a life together. He knew that she'd had a rough road and wanted to make life easier for her.

Some people like to tell each other all the details about their past relationships, but Louis preferred to live in the present moment. He didn't feel the need to know about Angela's old boyfriends, marriage, or divorce. That was fine with Angela, because none of the stories were good ones.

Louis liked Angela's children right away. He proposed to Angela after meeting the kids twice. He felt it was important to let Angela know that he was in with both feet—he wanted to make it official as soon as possible.

Louis had no idea how much Angela and her ex-husband Sam fought until after they had married and were living together. The divorced parents were worse at co-parenting than they had been at being married to each other. They argued about everything from the custody schedule to finances, extracurricular activities, and bedtimes. Louis would come home from work and see the dark cloud on the faces of the children, and he would know that Angela and their dad Sam had been arguing. After Angela had been talking with Sam, she was like a shaken can of soda.

"What happened, sweetheart? Do you want to talk about it? Can I help?" he would ask her gingerly.

"Nothing new," she'd bark, and "nothing for you to do." She would follow this by ordering the kids to do something or other and then would go into her room. You'd think that Louis and the kids might bond over these experiences—even share a look. But instead they all looked anywhere but at each other, uncomfortably trying to cope with the tension, each in their own way.

Routinely, Louis gave Angela about fifteen minutes and followed her into the bedroom. Angela would be crying or crabby, and he felt like he was walking on eggshells. At times, he felt as if he'd walked unawares into a war zone. But overtime, Louis's patience paid off, and he earned Angela's trust. She started talking with him about the problems with her ex-husband and found to her surprise that he had helpful ideas for handling the situation. Angela was not accustomed to turning to others for help.

The kids' attitudes toward their mom's new marriage ranged from lukewarm to unhappy. It was uncomfortable to have a man that they hardly knew living in their house and sleeping with their mom. Even though they hadn't liked the way their parents fought all the time, the divorce had been sad for them. And Louis's very presence symbolized the fact that their parents were not getting back together.

To some degree, Louis understood their feelings and knew that the relationships were going to take some time to develop. He tried to show interest in their activities. Too often, Louis would ask one of the kids a question that rubbed them the wrong way or they were just in a mood, and they would roll their eyes, glare, and stomp off into their bedroom, not coming come out again until they were hungry. Louis felt like the kids were taking their upset out on him, that his mere presence aggravated everyone, reminding them that the original family unit was broken.

Generally, Louis was a cheerful person, and he wanted to live in a positive environment. Louis tried his best to turn the other cheek whenever he could, even though his feelings had been hurt. He didn't like the way the problems between Angela and her ex-husband Sam put everyone in the family on edge. It would have been easy for Louis to team up with Angela and call Sam the villain. He definitely resented Angela's first marriage interfering with their new life together. But instead, he tried to help Angela think about things with her ex-husband a little differently.

He helped her to see Sam's perspective, and gave her honest feedback on how she was feeding their negative dynamic. Louis encouraged Angela to find a new way of relating to Sam. In time, as she shifted her perspective, Angela became a little less critical of her ex-husband as well as calmer and more disciplined with the children. She enjoyed having a new partner with whom she could communicate and who seemed to understand and accept her. Her pent-up frustration from her previous marriage began to heal, and she stopped yelling at her ex-husband when they had their differences. In return, Sam responded by becoming more available for cooperative co-parenting.

Children can be keen observers; they noticed Louis encouraging Angela to stop fighting with their dad. For example, when Sam would yell at Angela in front of the kids, or on the phone, Angela would normally yell back. They saw that when their parents fought in front of them, Louis would give Angela a look, and she would stop. She would make an effort to stay calm and matter of fact.

"We aren't going to figure this out by yelling, Sam. Let's talk later when we are both calmer," she'd say if a phone call became argumentative. If Sam didn't stop, she would hang up, saying that she couldn't do the yelling thing anymore and she'd talk after they had both calmed down. Slowly, they began talking to each other more civilly with much less hostility. The children began breathing a little easier. With Louis's influence, when Angela and Sam needed to discuss a problem, they tried to do it when the kids were not in hearing range. Being in the middle of their parents' mutual animosity had been a painful experience for the children. And they in turn appreciated how Louis was able to have a positive influence in their new family structure.

Points to Ponder

- As stepparents, we are stepping into an existing family structure and having to create a place for ourselves.
- In reality, we have very little control—especially in the beginning.
- We can look for opportunities to make a positive contribution.
- We should be open to feedback and proceed cautiously.
- It is possible to significantly affect the adjustment and wellbeing of our new family.

You can probably imagine just how opinionated I was as a psychologist about the way things should be in our family. And there have been times when my input or perspective has helped move my family in a positive direction. But just as often, I've needed to pause and check my ego, judgment, and training at the door. I have had to focus on accepting and finding peace with whatever was happening in the moment—and always determinedly returning to love. These are my best moments in my family: when I let go of my own intellectual process, open my heart, and step into the present energy of love.

In these increasingly complex times, maintaining a long-term relationship is challenging enough; when you add ex-spouses and children from previous marriages into the mix, making a happy life together can seem daunting. But it is possible. Many people have done it. And if you and your spouse are committed to doing so, you will find some tools here that can help you.

Becoming really great parents requires adults to develop a new level of maturity in which they care about the needs of another person more than their own. With healthy adults, there is a strong biological imperative to take care of your children. With stepparents, this innate wiring is a little weaker, because we didn't give birth to these children and in most cases we have not known them since they were babies. Successful stepparenting challenges us to take our character development to a higher level—to discipline ourselves to consider the importance of the parent–child relationship even when it may seem to undermine our own needs at times. I hope the stories and information included here will inspire and guide you toward becoming your best self. The experience of being a stepparent can be a teacher, giving us an opportunity to deepen our capacity to love.

According to the most recent statistics, blended families are rapidly outnumbering the traditional nuclear family. And second marriages with children have a 60–70 percent likelihood of ending in divorce. With this kind of success rate, it's a wonder that people keep trying; but we are social beings with a genetic imperative to bond. Thankfully, when it comes to love, hope springs eternal. Being a stepparent can provide an opening to love just for the sake of loving.

In his day, French philosopher Pierre Teilhard de Chardin (1881–1955) was known to say, "You are not a human being in search of a spiritual experience. You are a spiritual being immersed in a human experience." The idea that we all come from a universal source of energy seems more widely accepted today in conjunction with the broadening family structure. People have all sorts of names for this energy, such as love, nature, God, spirit, or consciousness.

Points to Ponder

- As stepparents, we play an important role in creating a family in which every member can thrive.
- When we choose to marry someone with children, thereby becoming stepparents, we make a commitment to our spouse and their children.
- Divorced families have had enough of instability and dysfunction; they need both partners to be committed and bring the best of ourselves to the table.

Many of you are seeking deeper meaning and happiness in your lives, and that was part of your decision to marry your current partner. There are not any quick fixes here; the aim is not superficial adjustment. But within these pages you will find methods based on scientific research as well as my clinical and personal experience for how to develop loving relationships and resiliency—skills that stepparents arguably need in order to live happily ever after.

For some stepparents, it may seem like you are stepping into a fractured family system and trying to make it whole again, in a different shape, while some family members may still be attached to the old family structure. Nevertheless, millions of stepparents are helping their new families to heal in various ways every day. You may feel you have very little control in your blended family. It's a tough balancing act to keep in mind the rights, needs, and wants of others while being true to your own self. Most divorced families have at least a little leftover baggage. When you marry someone who has had children with another adult with whom they can no longer live for whatever reason, there are bound to be complications. It's possible that you've never been in such a challenging situation before. I can't think of anything that motivates us to stretch and grow our character as much as true love.

Points to Ponder

- Many people believe planet Earth is a postgraduate university that we've willingly enrolled in—the curriculum being to improve the quality of our souls.
- The more awareness that we have of the spiritual path or presence within us that connects all of us to each other, the more our relationships and quality of life will benefit.
- Our perspective determines the view that we see.

Soul and Spirituality Defined

In his book *Care of the Soul: A Guide for Cultivating Depth and Sacredness in Everyday Life,* Thomas Moore writes about the idea that the care of the soul is different than self-improvement from an egocentric perspective. Our soul is more than our individual circumstances and ideas. The soul has to do with the depth of a person and his or her infinite connectedness with the larger societal soul and, ultimately, the soul of the world.

If we are patient and look hard enough, there is goodness to be found in everyone. There is a transformation happening around the globe—a shift in consciousness. Many people are weary of the wars being fought over religion and resources, and are seeking more enlightened ways of handling conflicts and life in general. In a way, you might think of your whole extended stepfamily as a microcosm of our global, international family. It is your opportunity to create a tiny island of peace in the world.

Our soul is a type of consciousness, which has to do with our level of awareness. All living beings have some type of awareness, whether it's physical, emotional, intellectual, transpersonal, or a combination. For example, some flowers open during the daytime and close at night. Whales and birds migrate in the same pattern every year, and sunflowers turn toward the sun. All living beings respond positively to love and negatively to fear; when we recognize this we can have compassion for the circumstances of others amidst the interconnected fabric of life.

One Human Family

When you feel like an outsider in your family, remind yourself of the positive ways you are connected to members of your family. For example, if you were to go back a thousand years in your family tree, you could have a million or more grandparents! Genealogy is the study or investigation of ancestry and family history. Genealogists claim that when we go back far enough, we will find that we are all eventually related. The Sorenson Molecular Genealogy Foundation is working on a project—the goal of which is to demonstrate just how closely we are all related. The foundation hopes to promote tolerance and peace by making people aware of our intricate ties. Their work is a reminder that we are all in a very real sense brothers and sisters.

Seven Key Components for Successful Stepparenting

- Commitment
- Love
- Self-awareness
- Empathy
- A good marriage
- Optimism
- Resiliency

Exercises:

1. Write down two positive qualities of each individual in your stepfamily; include your spouse, your children, your stepchildren, and the other biological parents.

_____

_____

_____

_____

_____

_____

_____

_____

_____

_____

_____

_____

_____

_____

_____

_____

_____

_____

_____

_____

_____

_____

_____

_____

_____

2. What are two things that you and your spouse can do to cooperate with the other biological parents of your children and stepchildren?

_____

_____

_____

_____

_____

_____

_____

_____

_____

_____

_____

_____

_____

3. What are some of your core values or spiritual beliefs that can help you cope and flourish as a stepparent?

_____

_____

_____

_____

_____

_____

_____

_____

_____

_____

_____

_____

_____

_____

_____

_____

_____

_____

_____

_____

_____

_____

_____

_____

_____

_____

_____

_____

_____

_____

_____

_____

_____

_____

Chapter Three

Taking Care of Your Marriage in a Blended Family

*"Marriage, ultimately, is the practice
of becoming passionate friends."*
—HARVILLE HENDRIX

When Neil and Sally married, they both had children from their previous marriages. Sally had a ten-year-old daughter named Sandy, and Neil had a thirteen-year-old son named Gregg. Gregg had always been a challenging boy. He had been a schoolyard bully in elementary school and went on to more delinquent behavior in middle school. He was angry about his parents' divorce and had taken to spending most of his time at his friends' houses. When he was home, he was rude and disrespectful to every member of the family. He would arrive home and stomp into his room without greeting anyone, and if they insisted that he speak or join them for dinner, he would be sullen and angry throughout the meal. Sally would insist that Gregg join them for dinner even though his dark mood clouded the experience for all of them. Neil had a more hands-off attitude and argued for leaving Gregg to sulk in his room. He didn't see the harm in letting Gregg fix himself a plate of whatever they were having and take it to his room. Sally saw that as letting Gregg get away with bad behavior. Neil figured it was a phase and that Gregg would get tired of it on his own. Neil and his ex-wife had Gregg in counseling, but it didn't seem to be helping very much.

To make matters worse, Gregg teased his little stepsister mercilessly. He'd call her dumb, ugly, fat—really anything that he thought might upset her. It was only when Sandy would cry or run to her room that they would see the rare smile come to Gregg's face. Sally and Sandy began staying away from the house as much as possible when Gregg visited. Arguments in their household became a regular thing. Sally wanted Neil to take away Gregg's privileges for bad behavior, and Neil wanted to carefully pick and choose his battles. He didn't want his son's time with him to be all about discipline; nevertheless, he sprinkled it in to appease his wife and to protect his stepdaughter.

Over time, Gregg found excuses to come around less and less. He got away with more at his mom's house, and he probably felt like odd man out at his dad's house. His mom hadn't remarried, and he pretty much called the shots at her house. She worked a lot and was too tired to fight with him when she was home. So Gregg got his way most of the time. Meanwhile his stepsister Sandy now lived with Gregg's dad eighty percent of the time and with her own dad twenty percent of the time. As result, Sandy lived with Gregg's dad substantially more than he did. This made Gregg feel more resentful and awkward at his dad's house. He felt like he was the intruder— an outsider. Of course, his behavior exacerbated things, but at age thirteen, his insight was understandably limited as to his role in his own difficulties. When at his dad's house, he was constantly scolded for being mean to Sandy. And justifiably so: he called her names; made fun of her and her friends; and would trip her or bump into her, roughly barking at her for being in the way. The less that Gregg came around, the less comfortable everyone felt when he did.

Neil felt like Sally was too hard on his son and Sally believed that Neil was too easy on him. Tensions seemed to heighten when they tried to discuss the situation, so they talked about it as little as possible and just soldiered through it. Layers of unresolved conflict began building up and creating walls between them. It became harder to deal with any challenging subjects, because they both reacted quickly with anger or they withdrew from each other. They both felt isolated and defensive, and the intimacy between them withered.

When Sally and Neil finally sought counseling, they had to muster the courage to talk about their disappointments and hurts with each other. Before Neil and Sally could rekindle their relationship, they needed to understand how each of them felt alienated and unsafe in their relationship. Sally felt that Neil was more concerned with his son's needs than with hers; Neil felt that Sally focused more on her daughter's individual needs rather than seeing the whole picture.

"I feel like you are more concerned about Gregg than you are about us," Sally explained. "I need you to protect Sandy from Gregg when he bullies her and correct him when he's disrespectful toward me. He's trying to sabotage our marriage, and you are letting him! Maybe you don't want this marriage. Maybe you'd rather go live somewhere alone with just you and your son." Sally broke into sobs—covering her face with her hands. Neil tried to reassure her.

"Honey, please." He tried to pry her hands away from her face so he could look into her eyes.

Sally pulled away angrily, yelling, "Stop it! You don't care about us!" And the fight was on.

Neil felt he had been sacrificing for Sally and Sandy; he was seeing his son quite a bit less by this time. Sally had insisted that Gregg mostly come over only on the days that Sandy was with her father.

"How can you even say that?" Neil shouted. "Do you want me to completely alienate my son? I have a responsibility to look out for him. Do you want me to completely stop being his dad? He's just a kid going through a tough time. I am his father, and I will not abandon him."

Sally softened upon seeing Neil's pain. "I know that you have made sacrifices to help Sandy and me feel comfortable. We really appreciate it. I don't mean to say that you haven't. But sometimes, I feel like you are more concerned with Gregg's needs than ours. I need to know that I am your number one priority. Of course, you have to take care of Gregg, but not at the expense of my daughter and me."

"What do you want me to do that I haven't already done?" Neil pleaded with her. "Really, what else can I do?" His hope for a happy second marriage was fading.

"You know what? I appreciate everything that you've done to help Sandy and me feel comfortable in our home. You are right. You've done a lot. I don't know what else you could do. But you are angry with me about it. I can tell. Something has changed in our relationship. You are really distant." Sally sighed.

"That's because I feel like whatever I do, it's not enough. Don't you think that it's painful for me to have these problems with my son? I feel terrible about it. But all you seem to be concerned about is the way you and Sandy feel!" Neil started getting louder in an effort to be heard.

Sally paused and then gently said, "That's because you don't tell me how you feel. You've never told me that it's painful for you. All I know is that I've had to fight for the changes every step of the way, and you seem to keep getting further and further away." Her hazel eyes were soft and teary. She appreciated Neil opening up to her. "You have done a lot for Sandy and me. I know that you are in a very difficult position. I think that you've been handling it well. It even seems like Gregg is a little more respectful—or maybe it would be more accurate to say, less disrespectful." She looked apologetic for possibly sounding critical. "My only real complaint these days is feeling like you are so far away. I know that you have taken me into consideration when you've made these decisions regarding Gregg and his time with us. And I'm getting that it's been really hard for you." She touched Neil's hand.

Neil had a hard time making eye contact. "It helps to hear that. I haven't felt that you've appreciated anything that I've done or how hard it is for me. Sometimes, I'm afraid that you are going to leave me like my ex did."

"When you feel far away, I'm afraid that *you* don't want to be with *me.* I don't want another divorce. I love you and want to be with you. I miss you and want to be close again." Sally moved closer to Neil.

"Then please don't ask me to choose between you and my son. I shouldn't have to. You are both important to me and it puts me in an impossible position. Can you understand that?" Neil looked at Sally.

"Yes," Sally said. "I don't want you to feel that way. I respect how you are trying to be a good father to Gregg and what a great husband and stepfather you've been to us."

As Neil and Sally practiced talking about their most vulnerable feelings they got better at sharing and listening to each other—they began to understand and respect each other at a deeper level. They started to feel safer and mutually supportive even though they still didn't always agree on how to handle things. And their problems were less likely to pull them apart. They both moved more toward the middle and worked hard together to find solutions that they could manage without resentment on either side.

Points to Ponder[1]

- The way a couple manages conflict is more important than the actual problems themselves.
- Underlying most marital conflicts is a sense of alienation or fear about losing your connection with your partner.
- Chronic lack of emotional engagement is a precursor for divorce.
- Learning how to reassure one another and respond to each other's needs is essential for making your marriage work.

As I have mentioned before (and will again), many of the conflicts that arise in stepfamilies have to do with the children. Biological parents tend to be more defensive about their own kids

---

1 The points in this list are distilled from the research and writings of John Gottman and Sue Johnson.

while stepparents may tend to be more critical. It's a little bit like you can say whatever you want about your own mother, but if someone else says it, even if they care about her too, it's different. Awareness of these differences can help you be more sensitive in the way you try to talk about complications when they inevitably arise.

- Studies indicate that the quality of a couple's friendship determines 70 percent of the satisfaction level for both men and women.
- Being able to trust that you and your partner are there for each other, no matter what, is an important part of making marriage work.
- When you bring adults and children from different parents together, there are bound to be conflicting needs—it's helpful if you can all find a balance between asserting yourself and making room for others.

Obviously, marriage becomes more complex when children are involved, and stepcouples have to manage this right from the start. Blended families begin with a multitude of mixed loyalties, with the needs of children and ex-spouses needing to be considered; this shortens and sometimes hinders having the traditional honeymoon period that newlyweds might anticipate.

Children Benefit When Their Parents Have High-Quality Marriages

Research has revealed happy people to be more kind and generous with others;[2] so naturally it follows that happily married couples will have more positive energy available for tending to their children. One of the major ways that children learn about relationships is by watching their parents. Children whose parents

---

2 Christopher Peterson and Martin E. P. Seligman, *Character Strengths and Virtues: A Handbook and Classification* (New York: Oxford University Press and Washington, DC: American Psychological Association, 2004).

have divorced can benefit from the modeling of healthy adult love relationships.

- United States Census Bureau statistics indicate that the higher divorce rates in second and third marriages (approximately 66 percent) are largely due to conflicts about the children.
- When the going gets tough, you can tap into your love for your partner to inspire your commitment to your stepchildren.
- A good marriage is the bedrock on which a healthy family relationship can be built.
- Although children are a top priority, the marital relationship needs to be of equal importance.

A Safe Emotional Harbor

"Compassion, loving kindness, altruism, and a sense of brotherhood and sisterhood are the keys to human development, not only in the future but in the present as well."
—THE DALAI LAMA

Stuart resented that his wife Melanie had to pay alimony to her ex-husband, who rarely saw the kids. Melanie felt trapped in her financial situation with her ex-husband. It only made it worse when Stuart brought it up. But Stuart was chronically frustrated because he wanted to do things as a family—like go on vacation. He wanted to pay for the family trip together and believed it would be a good bonding opportunity for his kids and his stepkids. But Melanie insisted that they couldn't afford it. It was a hot topic between Stuart and Melanie to the extent that when it came up, all of the kids would leave the room. For years, Stuart and Melanie couldn't talk about their feelings or ideas without the other person blowing a gasket. Neither of them felt comfortable discussing difficult subjects. Whenever they tried it they ended up in a fight. Eventually, alimony to Melanie's ex-husband and college expenses ended. Money ceased to be a bone of contention between Stuart and

Melanie. But the chronic arguing had taken a toll, and it took a lot of counseling to get the relationship back to a quality place.

Points to Ponder
- It's true that adults want some different things in relationships than children do.
- Just as children do, adults also need secure, loving attachments that provide comfort, connection, and a sense of belonging.
- As adults, we need a safe emotional harbor in our spouse.
- We need to feel safe with each other in order to experience and maintain a deep connection.

Second or third marriages where children are involved face more difficult challenges than first marriages for a number of reasons. One of the most common sources of tension is when the biological parent feels torn between a conflict among his children and his spouse. It takes time to gain one's balance and learn how to work as a stepcouple in a way that is healthy for the marriage and for the stepfamily.

How to Begin Feeling Safe with Your Partner
- Listen to one another's feelings and thoughts fully without interruptions and without judging each other.
- Avoid a "me versus you" or "us versus you" attitude—it breeds defensiveness, insecurity, and hostility.
- When we feel understood, we can loosen our grip on being right or wrong—our minds then become more open to new ideas.
- Take turns expressing yourselves.
- Take your turn only after your partner feels fully understood and try not to negate his or her perspective when expressing yours.

When you marry someone who has children, your spouse and his or her kids have a history and culture together of which you haven't been a part. There are priorities, rituals, styles of relating, and unspoken understandings that have been in place since long before you came on the scene. This can sometimes feel alienating. It takes time to create your own positive memories and rituals and become woven into the fabric of the family. The degree to which your new family is inclusive or exclusive will of course affect your adjustment and assimilation. Even blended families that welcome the stepparent wholeheartedly pose complications for adults who step into an already formed family.

According to Dr. John Gottman's research at the University of Washington, couples that accept influence from each other have more successful marriages. For example, a stepmother tells her husband that she thinks her stepdaughter needs an earlier curfew. Her husband can say that the existing curfew was in place long before she got there, or he can ask his wife to share her thoughts in more depth with him and then take these into consideration. When one partner accepts influence from the other, it inspires a sense of true partnership.

Points to Ponder
- When you are able to convey to your partner that his or her feelings are as important as your own, it can help him or her feel accepted and safe.
- This doesn't mean that you have to agree or acquiesce to what the other person wants.
- But ideally, through mutual understanding and good communication, you can both see that you have each other's best interest at heart and don't want to hurt each other.

Changing Boundaries
Biological parents often feel like they are caught in the middle between their new partner and their own child. Javier was happily remarried to Maria. Once they were engaged, Javier continued to have regular contact with his ex-wife Marsha. She called him with concerns about their children as well as to seek personal advice for

her self. Javier didn't think much of it. He just wanted everyone to be happy and to get what each of them wanted. Maria, however, felt Marsha was calling too often. It felt intrusive to her, as if Marsha were unwilling to let go of her ex-husband. Maria told Javier that Marsha was finding excuses to call him. It wasn't until they were on their honeymoon and Marsha called Javier to tell him that their daughter's earache was better (which Javier didn't even know she had) that Javier realized there might be a problem.

Women tend to be more territorial when it comes to their homes and families. While it can be understandably threatening for a woman with children to see her ex-husband (and often the financial provider postdivorce) moving on with another woman and family, healthy boundaries benefit everyone.

Javier had dismissed his new wife Maria's feelings as petty and unfounded jealousy. But if we talk about our differences in a nonconfrontational way, listen to each other and stay patient, over time almost anything can be worked out. Eventually, Javier began setting more limits with his ex-wife Marsha, who then began turning to her new husband more; this was better for her marriage also. It usually takes time for old family patterns from the prior marriage to shift to new habits. Healthy communication and accepting each other's influence can lead to beneficial boundaries for the family as a whole.

Taking a Time Out

- Couples who create boundaries early on in their relationships about the behaviors they will and will not tolerate have more successful marriages.
- Those unwilling to accept hurtful treatment from each other from the beginning of their relationship fare the best.
- Learning to repair, avoid, or exit an argument can prevent the disagreement from becoming destructive to the relationship.
- Taking a "time out" can help put an argument on pause while each partner gets hold of his or her temper.
- An individual's ability to reason and manage emotions is compromised in a state of fight or flight.

Once we get overly agitated, our fight or flight mechanism kicks in, sending adrenaline rushing through our bodies. If you and your spouse tend to have big emotional reactions or tempers, try making an agreement when things are calm between you. For example, you can agree that when you are in a state of conflict or upset with each other, either party can call a time out (usually somewhere between fifteen minutes and twenty-four hours long). It's important to agree that you won't chase each other in an attempt to engage but will both respect the agreement. During the time out, think about how you contributed to the escalation of the situation. When you and your partner do talk about it, tell him or her what you realized about your contribution. Tell him or her what you need and want using "I" statements rather than "you" statements. For example, "I need you to spend time with me," instead of "You never spend time with me!" It isn't realistic to expect that there won't be arguments (in fact, research indicates that couples who don't ever argue are more likely to get divorced).[3] Every family and couple has problems, some of which never completely go away. The key to success is how you handle those challenges together. When you can talk to each other with mutual respect, each accept influence from the other, maintain a sense of humor, and accept that things will never be absolutely perfect—your marriage has the ingredients for a passionate, lifelong friendship.

Managing differences in a constructive way (with acceptance and compromise)

> *All wars and conflicts arise out of not honoring*
> *the differences between others and ourselves.*
> —RUMI

All blended family issues get played out in the marriage. There is a myth in our culture that if we find our ideal soul mate,

---

3 John Gottman and Robert Levenson, "A Two-Factor Model for Predicting When a Couple Will Divorce: Exploratory Analyses Using 14-Year Longitudinal Data," *Family Process* 41, no. 1 (2002), 83–96.

we will be perfectly compatible. Differences are a normal part of married life, especially in stepfamilies. Again, it's how we handle our differences that can make or break a marriage. Do your best to bring up problems with sensitivity and without blame.

Torn Between My Guys

Following is a letter from and response to someone who wrote in to my advice column:

Dear Dr. Diana,

My 16-year-old son moved out a few months ago to live with his dad who never paid child support and was barely around. My son told us he was moving out with a nasty text. My husband (his stepdad) and I were angry and didn't let him come and get his stuff at first. Recently, my son started visiting us and his stepbrother and sister. His stepdad is angry with me for forgiving my son because he hasn't apologized. Even if he doesn't say so, I know he's sorry and I figure he's young.

My husband has always been jealous of my son, which has really bothered me. Now, he is so negative on my son, it makes me wonder if he

When you and your partner have different perspectives on something, try to make understanding each other's perspectives the first priority. We've all experienced someone arguing with us or minimizing our feelings or thoughts, and it makes us dig our heels in deeper, holding even more tightly to our own view of things. When we feel understood and accepted, the need to be right subsides and we tend to be more open to other vantage points. It must be human nature.

Pete and Joan both had children from previous marriages when they created their blended family. They were both devoted parents—their children came first. Once they were living together, they realized that their discipline styles were vastly different. Joan was strict and Pete was more laissez-faire. For example, if Joan's kids came in after curfew, they were grounded for the following weekend. If Pete's kids came in after curfew, he turned the other cheek and felt glad that he could trust them. He knew he had good kids, and they didn't seem to get into any trouble. They were polite and well-mannered for the most part.

ever really cared for him at all. I feel like I have to choose between my son and my husband. I am so confused and don't know what to do.

Caught in the Middle

Dear Caught in the Middle,

Relationships in stepfamilies can be complex. There are many different issues going on. Sometimes, absentee parents reappear on the scene when the children are a little older. Initially, some kids are eager to get to know their parent who has been distant—especially when they share the same gender. This may be especially painful to your husband, who probably has formed a genuine, caring bond with your son over the past eight years. So, rather than not caring, it may be that your husband is feeling more hurt than you'd think.

Biological parents often feel like they are caught in the middle between their spouse and their child. And kids often feel like they are caught between their divorced parents. Meanwhile,

He always gave them the benefit of the doubt. It drove Joan crazy that he didn't enforce the curfew. It became a real problem when their kids were at the same party and had the same curfew. Joan's kids would come home on time, but their stepsiblings would come home late without suffering any consequences. Naturally, Joan's kids started resenting the rules. Additionally, all the kids were supposed to clear their plates and clean up together, but Joan's kids ended up doing the lion's share of the work. They complained bitterly to their mom, who tried to get her stepkids to help with their chores. When they didn't respond, she took it up with her husband. It was a real point of contention.

Eventually, they reached a compromise of sorts. They had a few minor household rules (like everyone takes their plate to the sink after dinner). Each parent was responsible for handling enforcement of the rules with his or her own kids. Pete wouldn't discipline Joan's children, and Joan wouldn't discipline his. The kids had to deal with the differences and accept their lot. Complaining didn't get them anywhere. Joan and Pete tried not to judge each other's approaches, even though it was difficult. Over the years, they learned from watching each *pre-existing histories and loyalties among children and parents can make the stepparent feel like a third wheel or a second-class citizen in his or her own home. Children, in turn, may be fearful that they will lose some of their parent's attention or love to the stepparent.*

People marry and make families in part to have a sense of belonging. We all want to feel like our loved ones care about our feelings— to feel that we matter to them. In our relationships with our children, there is an innate protective instinct that defies words. With our romantic partners, the attachment is different. But the need to be understood and accepted and to have a secure sense of belonging is consistent across different types of relationships in the family. So, when a parent is preoccupied with the needs of a child, and perhaps not as aware of how his or her partner is being affected, it can feel threatening and alienating to the partner.

At any rate, it might help your husband's upset if you take some time to acknowledge his anger and hurt. Let him

other. Eventually, the chasm between their different styles became smaller.

Points to Ponder

- When couples make mutual acceptance and respect a higher goal than being right or wrong, disagreements have a much shorter shelf life.

- When partners can argue without being disrespectful or destructive, they can develop a creative marriage and model these skills for their children.

- For most kids from divorced families, their opportunities to observe adults handling conflicts well have been infrequent.

Being Nice to Each Other

"It is not a lack of love, but a lack of friendship that makes unhappy marriages."
—FRIEDRICH NIETZSCHE

As stepparents, we have the opportunity to model a marriage that inspires our children to be considerate, loving, family-oriented individuals. Happily married couples are nice to each other. They go out of their way to do nice things. According to John Gottman's research at the University of Washington, the ratio of positive to negative experiences in happy couples *know that you understand and appreciate his feelings and all the efforts that he's made in the past. You can agree with him—neither of you approve of how your son handled things, but you need him to respect your decisions about how you want to handle the situation. It's very likely that at the root of your husband's anger is protectiveness toward you. He may be concerned that if your son is not overtly apologetic or remorseful, that he will repeat the behavior and hurt you again. It's very likely that if you express your appreciation of his patience and tolerance throughout this difficult situation, his frustration may subside. When we feel that our partner understands us, accepts us and has our back, we feel more secure and generous.*

is twenty happy experiences for every one negative experience. In conflicted but relatively healthy couples, it is five positive experiences to one negative experience; and in soon-to-divorce couples it is eight negative experiences for every positive experience. For every negative experience a couple shares, it takes five positive experiences to neutralize it. For example, if I am short tempered with my husband and it hurts his feelings, it will take five positive experiences to neutralize my moment of irritability.

It helps if you know what your partner likes and needs. Susan made sure that the house was always stocked with what everyone needed. She made nice meals for all of their kids and had dinner ready when her husband Joe came home in the evening. She kept a clean house. She worked a part-time job (their children were young) so that she could help out financially. And yet, her husband Joe was irritable toward her and repeatedly told her that she wasn't meeting his needs—he didn't feel cared about. Susan felt that taking care of his kids demonstrated to him how much she cared and was frustrated because she was trying to show him how much she appreciated him and was there for him. The problem was that the nice things that she was doing were not the ones that mattered to him. Of course he appreciated her efforts, but she was exhausted from everything she was trying to do perfectly and had nothing left for him at the end of the day. He missed their earlier friendship and intimacy. For example, he would have preferred that she bring in takeout and have time to sit with him and talk about their days. He wanted to be intimate at nighttime, but she was worn out from the day.

Points to Ponder
- Take time to find out what your partner really wants from you; otherwise you can waste your efforts.
- It is a gift to have a partner who wants to learn what your specific needs and wants are—choose to be that partner.
- Of course, it is important to know what the specific needs and wants of your children and stepchildren are as well.

"I can't take it anymore," Felicia said emphatically. Albert sat quietly, his lips pursed tightly together. His face was flushed, revealing the strong feelings coursing through his veins. "I feel terrorized when your children are at our house. I stay in my room and feel like a prisoner in my own home. I don't want our child growing up and seeing his mother treated so disrespectfully—and his father standing by, letting it happen."

"I understand," Albert said again. "They treat me even worse. But they are my children, and I am their father. I don't know what I'm supposed to do."

Albert's ex-wife had not wanted the divorce. When Albert started dating Felicia, his ex-wife falsely confided in the children that Felicia was the cause of their parent's breakup. She told the kids that their dad had been seeing Felicia all along. This was not the case, but Albert's children believed their mother. They were angry with their father and despised their stepmother. Albert's kids called their dad, his wife, and their baby nasty names. Albert was concerned about the psychological damage being inflicted on his children and saw them as innocent bystanders in a war zone. Felicia understood that her husband was in a difficult spot. He only had his children 20 percent of the time, and as often happens, he didn't want to alienate them by disciplining them.

Once their baby came along, Felicia's attitude changed. "I can't tolerate your children being so rude, messy, and disrespectful in our home. I don't want our children following in their footsteps!"

Albert and Felicia bickered back and forth about how to handle the situation until Albert sadly conceded that his wife's request was reasonable. He didn't want to hurt his children, but he knew that he had to teach them that it wasn't okay to behave the way they had been. Albert and Felicia agreed on a firm and calm approach aimed at setting boundaries for appropriate behavior and a withdrawal of certain privileges for not following the rules. With this change, Albert's two oldest kids started coming over less and less, but the younger ones adapted better than expected, and their relationships improved.

Points to Keep in Mind When Conflicts Arise

- Biological parents often feel caught between their loyalties to their spouse and to their children.
- It's not a competition for love—it's about mutual respect.
- Your marriage needs to be protected and considered as a high priority.
- Prioritize mutual consideration when it comes to decision making.

Tips for Making Your Marriage Strong

- Do your best to cultivate and maintain a safe, secure relationship with your spouse and stepchildren.
- Practice good communication skills.
- Remember that the way you discuss conflict is more important than resolving conflict.
- Listen respectfully and empathize with each other's point of view.
- Be respectful of each other's feelings and needs.
- Remember the 20:1 ratio: happy couples have at least twenty positive experiences to every negative one.
- Create positive moments.
- Appreciate each other's strengths and focus on them more than the weaknesses.

EXERCISES

1. Write down some of your most positive early memories with your partner.

_____

_____

_____

_____

_____

_____

_____

2. Sit down with your partner and ask him or her for specific, concrete behaviors that you can do that would make him or her feel safe and loved. This can be as simple an unsolicited hug or opening a car door as you might have done when you were dating. Write it down so you will remember. Keep the list nearby and check it often.

_____

_____

_____

_____

_____

_____

_____

3. List five things that you appreciate about your partner. Then share your list with your partner.

_____

_____

_____

_____

_____

_____

4. If you want to, write down three things that are frustrating you right now about your partner.

_____

_____

_____

_____

_____

_____

_____

5. Now, write down a positive action or request for your partner that corresponds with each frustration.

_____

_____

_____

_____

_____

_____

_____

Chapter Four

Not All Love is Equal

"Him that I love, I wish to be free—even from me."
—ANNE MORROW LINDBERGH

Stepsibling Crush

Following is a letter from and response to someone who wrote in to my advice column:

Dear Dr. Diana,

My husband and I have been together for five years and married for two. This may sound paranoid, but I'm afraid that my seventeen-year-old stepson is attracted to my fifteen-year-old daughter. He stays with us every other week, and lately they have been spending a lot of time

There are many different kinds of love, including love for a child, romantic love, and a universal spiritual love for other human beings. The Dalai Lama, spiritual leader of the Tibetan people, describes *unconditional love* as "attitudes and actions that rise above emotional attachment. Emotions can ebb and flow from moment to moment— but unconditional love is not about feelings so much as a decision and commitment." In blended families, I think that cultivating an attitude of "unconditional love" toward all family members can be a helpful approach.

together whenever he is here. My daughter is not allowed to date, but she and her stepbrother have been going to the movies and grabbing dinner together. At first, we were thrilled that they were bonding like this, but I'm starting to get worried. My husband is offended that I'm afraid that his son might do something inappropriate with my daughter. I think that they like each other more than as stepsiblings and friends. I don't want to upset everyone, but can't just let this go on. Do you have any suggestions? —Suspecting Mother & Stepmother

Dear Suspecting,

Quite a pickle, assuming that your daughter and stepson have affection for each other that is more than platonic. Stepsiblings do sometimes become good friends, so it may be just that. We tend to hear more about stepsiblings who don't get along, but some stepsiblings do become fast friends—it may be that they have developed a special bond that is innocent enough.

In addressing this concern of yours, the focus really needs

The Dalai Lama talks about a type of compassion that neatly parallels the concept of unconditional love. First, he distinguishes between two different types of compassion. One type of compassion stems from a feeling of friendship and closeness; the other he calls "genuine compassion." The first tends to be unstable, because it is based on emotional attachment. If we become upset or hurt with a friend, the compassion toward that person may be replaced with feelings of anger or even hatred. "Genuine compassion" is free of personal attachment. It is based on the belief that all human beings have a natural desire and right to try to be happy and overcome suffering. Practicing genuine compassion can help us to create a sense of harmony with all other human beings. We are all members not only of our own immediate families, but part of the larger human family. We are all connected.

This idea brings to mind a story related by a woman—and stepmother; she had just moved from the United States to Argentina, where she experienced an unusual vision. All of the people in her new town seemed to be connected by ropes emerging from their belly buttons. She described what looked to her like ropes of energy linking the townspeople from *to be that your daughter isn't yet ready to date. It doesn't sound like your suspicions are necessarily personal to your stepson. It could help to make that crystal clear to everyone involved. If you haven't noticed any funny business or flirtation between these two kids, it's likely that they are platonic friends who happen to be stepsiblings. Usually adolescent girls start acting a little different when they get involved romantically with a boy. If you've noticed your daughter primping a little more, or her mood changing when your stepson is around, you may have some cause for concern.*

As you know, the art of parenting requires a delicate balance between setting limits and giving kids enough room to grow. At some point, we need to trust that we've imparted good values to our children. Cultivating a trusting, intimate relationship with your daughter in which she feels comfortable confiding in you can give you more influence in her life. If you haven't had the birds and the bees talk with your daughter then that is a good place to

one belly button to another. She also described seeing an energy stream that came from people's mouths when they spoke to one another. She said the energy ranged in color from amber honey to black bile. She realized that the amber color accompanied kind and sweet sentiments while the black bile represented fear or anger. At first, she kept this vision to herself because she feared that people would think that she was crazy. I am grateful she chose to share it with me. Whatever you think about her experience, it is an excellent metaphor for the reality that we are all made up of energy and connected with each other.

The feeling and attitude behind the words we speak are critical components to any communication. Imagine if others saw the underlying emotions or real meaning behind your words as different colors. What colors do you think would be streaming from your mouth at any given time? If you are aware of the intention and energy behind your words, you will find that people seem to respond accordingly.

Accepting your partner's children and treating them with kindness and respect can help to build this as a culture in your family. We need to be honest with ourselves. If we are going through the motions of love but we don't genuinely feel it, the children *start. By age fifteen, she's probably pretty well informed and she may think you're silly, but forge on until you find some common ground together. Afterward, you can ask her about her relationship with her stepbrother. Be diplomatic and curious rather than accusing.*

As strange as it sounds, since your daughter and stepson are not related by blood, at some point in the future if they do become interested in each other it won't be as incestuous as it might seem. But for the present moment, considering the fact that adolescent flirtations and romances are usually short-lived, it could become awkward for the family if these two are involved and then have a falling out. This is a practical perspective that you can share with your daughter and your stepson if they indeed do have special feelings for each other.

will not trust us. They can detect the absence of authenticity. If you don't feel love, try to practice kindness and respect toward them. These are the foundations of friendship, humanity, and love.

Kari married Roy when his son, William, was twelve years old. Six months after the wedding, William began living with them full time. His biological mother had emotional problems and was unable to care for the boy. When he was living with his mother, William had fended for himself, eating junk food for meals, sleeping random hours, and skipping school on a regular basis. When he moved in with Roy and Kari, he was unaccustomed to rules or structure of any kind.

Initially, William was depressed and withdrawn. But gradually, he began to blossom. Roy was devoted to his son. He also felt guilty about the divorce and the neglect that the boy had endured with his ill mother. Roy continued to be kind and caring toward his ex-wife even though he was very disappointed in how she had neglected their son. Roy's attitude of genuine compassion toward William's mother helped minimize any feelings of conflict that William might have had when he started spending more time with his dad and stepmom.

Meanwhile, Kari happily waltzed into the role of mother to William. Both males appreciated her cooking, cleaning, and nurturing. But the boy and his father fiercely rejected any other input regarding the parenting of William. Kari grew more hurt and frustrated as this pattern became even more fixed in the ensuing months. Her feelings of anger interfered with her ability to have compassion and patience with her stepson and husband. She sought counseling for her upset and feelings of alienation.

Kari realized that in her childhood family, she never felt that anyone respected or welcomed her opinions or feelings. Her experience in her new family had opened old wounds. Over time, she realized that her husband disagreeing with her didn't mean that he respected her opinions any less. It's just that he felt strongly about his own. In her counseling, Kari worked at respecting her own thoughts and feelings regardless of whether others agreed with her perspective or not. This made it easier for her to handle it when Roy had different views. Her attitude softened during their discussions because she realized that her hurt was coming from old injuries; with the hard edge gone, Roy was able to hear his wife's perspective better and take it into consideration. She found that the more compassion and respect she had for herself, the more genuine compassion she had for her husband and stepson. She was more open to Roy's ideas, and her heart didn't shut down when they disagreed. She accepted Roy's need to be the main parent and decision maker when it came to his son. Once she stopped trying to discipline or parent William, their friendship flourished. Her capacity to love herself, her husband, and her stepson deepened with her new understanding and acceptance.

Will You Be There for Me When Things Go Right?

The way we respond to someone else's good news can enhance our relationship or cause alienation.[4] If your stepchildren share something with you that they feel excited about, responding enthusiastically and showing your own excitement will promote

---

4 Shelly L Gable, Gian C. Gonzaga, and Amy Strachman, "Will You Be There for Me When Things Go Right? Supportive Responses to Positive Event Disclosures," *Journal of Personality and Social Psychology* 91, no. 5 (2006): 904-17.

Realistic Love for Stepparents

Following is a letter from and response to someone who wrote in to my advice column:

Dear Dr. Diana,

I was an unwed, young single mom. When I married my husband, my son was fifteen years old and his daughters were eight and ten. I was so excited to have a real family and have daughters. Six years later, things haven't turned out as I'd hoped. My son is away at college, and my stepdaughters are teenagers. I have tried to be the best stepmother that I could even though it's been difficult. My faith is strong, and love has always been my motto. But even though I've tried to be kind and patient all these years, my relationship with my stepdaughters is still very strained.

My husband says that they are teenagers and that is all it is. He thinks that our relationships will get better as they get older. But lately, I've been losing hope. I'm also frustrated that my husband isn't more assertive with his

a positive connection with them. This may seem obvious, but so often we are distracted by concerns or criticisms that we might have. It's best to wait until you have celebrated their accomplishment with them before you carefully express other thoughts or feelings.

When you do express concern, doing so in the form of questions can make it easier for the listener to accept your input. For example, sixteen-year-old Jenny had been looking for a summer job. She excitedly told her stepmother Jane that she had finally been hired—by the ice cream and hamburger fast-food chain Fosters Freeze. Jenny had a serious weight problem that was beginning to interfere with her social life, and Jenny and Jane had started going to Weight Watchers two weeks earlier.

Jane jumped out of her chair, matched the energy in Jenny's voice and congratulated her with a big hug. Jane asked Jenny to tell her all about it. After she heard all the details and delighted in the twists and turns of events, Jane asked Jenny a question on a different note.

"I'd find it hard to work somewhere like that and not eat the food all the time. Are you at all worried about that, honey? Do you think it will be hard to be around all that food?" Then

ex-wife. She speaks badly about him to their daughters and makes it difficult for us to see them. When we do have them, she interrupts our time by calling them constantly. Does this kind of situation ever really change, or do I need to adjust my expectations and accept that this is how things will always be?
—Wanting to Be a Realist

Dear Aspiring Realist,

Often, wishing that things were different than they are causes us the most pain. So, yes, I think it's a great idea to adjust your expectations accordingly and accept that this is how things are now. None of us know how things will be in the future. Anything can happen at any time. The best thing that you can do is exactly what you have been doing: take the high road and be a kind and stable presence in the lives of your stepchildren (you don't need to be a saint—you're only human—but just do your best). Depending on the individual personalities of your stepdaughters, your relationships may bloom once they have moved away from home and are on their own.

they talked about it. Jenny could feel Jane's love for her and therefore didn't feel defensive.

Jenny agreed that it wasn't ideal, but she really wanted a job and it was the only one she had found so far. They agreed that Jenny would take the job and keep looking for another. Before long, Jenny found a job taking tickets at a movie theatre and quit her job at the fast-food joint.

Jenny felt her stepmother's unwavering support, and consequently she was more open to Jane's guidance. Jane had been very gentle and thoughtful in her approach to guiding and supporting Jenny. She had clarity and peace of mind that she had cultivated over time. When your intentions come from the heart, other people pick up on that.

Most spiritual and religious traditions teach a type of meditation and prayer particular to them. Find the one that is right for you. Taking time to quiet our minds can cultivate inner calm and balance. To be a stable and loving presence in the lives of our stepchildren, we need to take good care of ourselves. Meditation or silent prayer can boost your immune system, reduce blood pressure, and decrease obsessive thinking and other compulsive habits. It can help you get in touch with

Just for the record, relationships between stepmothers and stepdaughters tend to be especially challenging. When fathers remarry, girls tend to be more territorial and competitive with their stepmother than boys are. Girls may also identify with their mother and feel more conflicted about bonding with their stepmother—feeling that if they do so, they are betraying their mother. In these cases, the nicer the stepmother is, the more it can kick up these issues for the kids. It's a tricky balancing act between showing affection and interest and giving them the space they need—assuming that you can accurately figure that out. Sometimes, the situation requires the mother to give her blessing and encouragement for her daughters to be open to a relationship with their stepmother. In your case, it sounds like their mother is still angry, which keeps the girls in the middle. It's probably very uncomfortable for them as well.

With divorce, no matter how much a stepparent or biological parent tries, the relationships can at times continue to be strained. This

a deep and quiet place in yourself. Sometimes we have beliefs, thoughts, and emotions that cause us to react in destructive ways. Setting aside time to clear away the confusion can promote self-awareness, open our hearts, and help us to offer a type of unconditional love. Below are some exercises to help you open your heart and clear away the troubled thoughts that can crowd out absolute or unconditional love.

EXERCISES

1. Start by sitting quietly for sixty seconds to five minutes and paying attention to the stillness deep inside you. Once you notice it, remember that deep peace is always there. You just have to tap into it.

2. Listen to music or seek out environments that open your heart to nature or beauty. It is calming and healing.

3. Think of someone who is easy for you to love. Breathe in your feelings for that person through your heart (I know it sounds strange, but try it). This will calm your nervous system and open your heart. This allows you to extend your positive heart energy to the person in front of you. This exercise can also help you to regulate your

can be especially painful for biological fathers who have lost time with their kids after the original family broke up. The frustration you feel when your husband doesn't stand up to his ex-wife is understandable; but with high-conflict people, confrontation doesn't always work. He's probably learned to pick and choose his battles carefully.

Bottom line: Being a stepparent (or a biological parent, for that matter) confronts us with the impossibility of controlling life. All we can do is rise to the occasion and be our best. Sometimes, this requires us to alter our expectations, pull back, or change course. But ultimately, you should continue to love your stepdaughters in your own way, because that is who you are and what you want to experience. Always come back to that as your rudder—and it will help you find your way.

emotions in a stressful situation (for more information on this approach, check out www.heartmath.com).

4. Repeating the following meditation to yourself can be enormously helpful. If you find sitting meditation too difficult, you can do a walking meditation. If meditation is not for you, try saying the words below a few times while you are driving or anytime you think of it. Most likely, you will find yourself taking deep, relaxing breaths as you repeat the following words to yourself:

> *"May I be filled with loving kindness."*
> *"May I be well."*
> *"May I live in peace and ease."*
> *"And may I be happy."*

5. After doing the above meditation for a few months, you may want to then practice the following:

> *"May all beings be filled with loving kindness."*
> *"May all beings be well."*
> *"May we all live in peace and ease."*
> *"And may we be happy."*

After doing this for a little while, notice how it changes your feelings toward yourself and others.

Chapter Five

Managing Stress

"Be still, breathe, know you are fine."
—JODIE PRESTON, MD

In the early days of their marriage, Phil and Ruby fought a lot. They both had children from previous marriages, and their situation was especially complex. They found themselves in constant conflict around their children and stepchildren. He thought she spoiled her children, and she thought he spoiled his. They both saw their stepchildren as manipulative and were defensive about their own children. Each of them had been hurt and disappointed in previous love relationships; they both felt safer clinging to their children, who might be less likely to abandon them than their new partner might be.

When Phil and Ruby got into a fight, they would hurt each other's feelings, and keep upping the ante. Phil would say something hurtful to Ruby, and she would try to hurt him back. Phil might say, "If I'd known that you'd be like this, I'd have thought triple time about marrying you."

To which a crushed Ruby would retaliate, "Look who's talking! Maybe I'll just leave now. If this is how it's going to be, I'm better off without you!"

And Phil would say, "Then leave! And leave your keys on the counter when you go because if you leave, you are not welcome back!"

They would keep trying to top each other, raising the stakes in who could hurt the other person more. It's a type of fight or flight reaction when your adrenaline starts pumping and you feel like you have to win or die.

One time when things got really hot and out of control and they were both threatening divorce, Ruby crumpled to the ground and cried softly, "I am in pain. I need your help." This immediately took the argument out of the realm of right versus wrong. Phil knelt beside her and asked what he could do. Ruby sobbed that she needed them to stop fighting and hurting each other, that she felt devastated at the thought of not being together. Phil softened and was able to respond to Ruby with a hug and sincere reassurance that he loved her and wanted to make it better.

Our society teaches us that dependency in adults is a sign of weakness; but the truth is that we need each other. As human beings, we are wired for social connection. Our physiology tells us that maintaining secure relationships is a matter of life and death. Human infants and small children die if left to survive alone; this is deeply embedded in our brains—attachment to others is a deep survival mechanism. It feels like life or death when our emotional connection feels threatened.

Phil and Ruby began to recognize that when they fought, they were usually feeling hurt and scared. They learned to take "time outs" when their tempers were flaring. Our brains can actually freeze up when we are emotionally upset, making it difficult to be rational and process information accurately.

Phil and Ruby started realizing that most of the time their arguments were less about a particular issue than about how they were treating each other. When they made a point of respecting and caring about the other's thoughts and feelings, even in the heat of the moment, almost anything could be figured out.

The better we are at managing stress, the more we can learn from the challenges that come our way. When children hear that one of their parents is getting remarried, they are confronted with the reality that their parents aren't getting back together. The stepparent then becomes a living reminder of their parents' divorce. It's not uncommon for stepparents to take the brunt of other people's disappointment and hurt. At these times, stepparents can avoid taking things too personally if they keep in mind the true source of the children's pain. We can grow through adversity by learning not to take others' feelings personally when those emotions are misdirected at us.

One of your best insulators against stress as a stepparent is the loyalty and commitment of your spouse. If the two of you stick together and do not let divisive issues come between you, everything will be easier. Good relationships are the regulators of physiological health. If children see their parents as a solid unit, they will also be more likely to feel secure. When couples fail to manage their stress effectively and to work together as a team, their marriage can suffer. Here are a few interesting facts compiled by the United States Census Bureau:

- About 75 percent of divorced persons eventually remarry.
- At least 65 percent of remarriages involve children from a prior marriage and form a blended family.
- 60–70 percent of all remarriages eventually end in legal divorce. Untold others will experience emotional divorce and unsatisfying relationships.
- More than 40 percent of all current marriages in the United States are second and third marriages.
- Blended families are now more common than traditional nuclear families in the United States.

Managing stress well is of course a central component of strong relationships, health, happiness, and good parenting. Some stress is good because it can push you beyond your usual limits.

For example, a deadline can push you to improve your focus and productivity. Or a loved one or a child in need can help you access energy that you didn't know you had. But when you feel chronically stressed or hopeless about things ever getting better, this state of mind can damage your health and your relationships. The mind and body are in constant communication with each other. Their synergy produces our experiences; that is, our thoughts trigger chemical and hormonal secretions, which in turn influence the way our bodies feel and function. The complexities of blended family relationships increase the chance that your buttons will be pushed; negative reactions can then trigger a series of stress responses in your body. If you don't believe your thoughts can cause physiological reactions, try this exercise: Close your eyes and pretend you are biting into a lemon. Taste the tart juice of the fruit. As you do this, notice how your mouth starts to salivate as if it's really happening.

If you are distressed or tweaked by some event or interaction in your family, it can trigger worries about the implications of the situation on your future. When you worry, what are you doing? You are imagining the worst possible scenario that could happen in a future moment. When you do that, your body experiences the negative situation as if it's happening right then, just like with the lemon. So, if you tend to always be expecting the other shoe to drop, anticipating negative events to occur, your body will experience these potential stressors as if they are actually happening. Your fearful thoughts can trigger the fight or flight response, which is a wired-in survival instinct. Chronic stress can cause serious wear and tear on your body as well as exhaust your mind. Worrying about the past or the future steals precious mental and emotional bandwidth that could be applied to this moment.

The Relaxation Response as a Remedy

There are a number of ways to soothe yourself and focus on the present moment instead of the past or future. The relaxation response is one of the body's natural healing mechanisms. The simplest way to trigger the relaxation response, the counterbalance to the stress reaction, is to quiet your mind and focus on either one word or noticing your breath. It's impossible to think while you are focused on breathing.

Set aside five minutes each day and try a relaxation or mindfulness exercise—you will notice that any tendencies that you have to be emotionally reactive will slow down. Chances are good that you will feel calmer and more at ease in your life.

Meditation helps activate areas in the brain associated with judgment and self-regulation. It helps bring the mind and body into a synchronized, healthy balance. At the end of this chapter, you'll find simple exercises designed to trigger the relaxation response and calm your mind, body, and spirit.

Julia met Howard a year after his divorce. There was still a lot of divorce recovery muck floating in the mix, and she became concerned about the future of her relationship with Howard. As a family man, he had not wanted to get divorced; it was his wife's idea. At times, Julia felt Howard put his children's or his ex-wife's concerns above her own. Howard felt guilty about the divorce, and it took him a few years to straighten out the boundaries with his ex-wife. This isn't unusual when people have ended long-term marriages. Their mindset doesn't immediately change just because living arrangements and paperwork are different. It's a stressful event for everyone concerned, and it takes time for new and healthy boundaries to be established by all parties concerned.

Julia readily admitted that she was insecure and impatient. She wanted to marry Howard and start a family of her own. As Julia and Howard grew closer, his ex-wife started having second thoughts and attempted to get her husband back. It was a very stressful period for both Howard and Julia—resentments between them started to build. Julia felt that Howard was allowing himself to be manipulated by his ex-wife in ways that interfered with their life together. She felt threatened and insecure, worrying she could lose her relationship with Howard and the stepchildren; she had grown to love them. He complained that she was unreasonable and rigid. Julia created distance from Howard and his children when she was scared. The reality was that they both needed to develop more empathy for each other; eventually they did, which allowed them to meet somewhere in the middle.

When Julia realized her relationship with Howard was on solid ground, she was able to work on her own stress reactions. She became aware that sometimes she worked herself up by merely thinking about the worst-case scenario (also known as worrying), rather than because something negative was actually happening in the moment. She started cultivating awareness of her own thought process and how this played into her stress reactions. When she found herself dwelling on past negative events or fears for the future, she refocused her attention on cultivating the positive aspects of her relationship with Howard in the present moment instead. Because whatever we focus on expands, the situation improved as Julia worked on building their strengths as a couple rather than dwelling on their weaknesses.

Blended family life is ripe with opportunities for pettiness, jealousy, competitive feelings, and turf wars. Sometimes it is best to take the high road and rise above these feelings, while at other times assertiveness and boundary setting is required. Knowing which path to take in each instance involves some individual soul-searching and frank discussion with one's spouse. As a rule, *a main diet of self-sacrifice does not work* because most of us start feeling resentful if we continually put our own needs aside and focus entirely on other people.

What Is Stress Really About?

Essentially, there are two different kinds of stress—external and internal. External has to do with outside events or situations happening to us. Internal stress often comes from our perception— the way we see a situation. Obviously, we only have so much control over external stressors. For example, we can make a point of being on time for appointments because it's less stressful not to rush. But we don't have as much control over unexpected changes in our schedule related to stepchildren or other people. But when it comes to the way we think about things that happen or how much we are going to worry or feel afraid, we have a choice.

A good rule of thumb is that when something upsets you, rather than dismissing it, examine your thoughts about the situation and compare these thoughts as logically as you can to the objective reality of the situation. If the stress has to do with another person, take some time and think about what the other person's point of view might be. Does putting yourself in his or her shoes change your perspective? For example, when Julia really tried to get past her own feelings and understand Howard's perspective, she found his position somewhat more palatable. Sometimes, it can help to talk with a fair-minded, trusted, and supportive friend about your thoughts and interpretations of the events in your world. Your friend may help you broaden your perspective at times and offer you a kind ear the rest of the time. Social support is an important antidote for stress. Everything is relative. The ability to shift our perspective, to see something from a different angle, can help us cope and even flourish within unsettling experiences.

The Dalai Lama's perspective on being forced to leave his native country, Tibet, and go into exile in India offers a good lesson for stepparents adjusting to their spouse, stepchildren, and extended family. He describes the interesting opportunities that have arisen from being a refugee in a foreign land. While he obviously wouldn't have chosen to experience the ongoing conflicts between his homeland and neighboring China, he appreciates certain aspects of his circumstances. An example that he gives is that since living in India, he has met many people from different religious backgrounds and walks of life that he would probably never have gotten to know if he were not in exile from his native land.

When problems arise in your blended family, try to find a perspective on the situation that is useful to you. If you find yourself focusing too much on the problem, so that it absorbs you without any constructive resolution in sight, it may be time to stop thinking about the problem, to give it a rest. For example, if you are frustrated about a certain aspect of how your stepchildren are being raised but there is nothing constructive that you can do about it at the moment, put your focus elsewhere. The Dalai Lama offers a practical suggestion: "If however, in spite of your efforts, you do not find any such positive angles or perspectives to a person's act, then for the time being the best course of action may be to simply try to forget about it."

At times, adjusting to life in a blended family can be overwhelming. Symptoms such as sleep disturbances, decreased energy, changes in appetite, anxiety, depression, inability to concentrate, and hopelessness may warrant further evaluation by a healthcare professional. For both children and adults, the stress of adjusting to a new set of family members can manifest in a variety of physical and psychological ways. Physical symptoms may include fatigue, difficulty "getting going," and stress-related complaints.

In order to be a stable and healthy member of your family, you'll need to find a way to keep a steady rudder and not get blown too far off course by the winds of your own reactions to the people around you. It's natural to feel left out and to have other uncomfortable emotions at times; the key is how you manage your own feelings and perceptions.

Emotions are a type of energy that you experience in your body. Sadness is often felt in the chest and throat area. In extreme cases, it can feel like someone is sitting on your chest—a sense of crushing heaviness. When you are angry you probably feel a surge of energy coming up through your body into your throat. Some people learned as children to ignore their feelings because they weren't allowed to express anger or there wasn't anyone around to support the emotions they experienced. The smartest coping strategy that they had was to cut off their feelings and go numb. But that doesn't make the feelings go away, it just bottles them up inside. All that pent-up emotional energy can then erupt in a weak moment, in a temper flash or crying episode. It can also come out in physical problems such as headaches, stomachaches, backaches, or fatigue. Holding in your feelings too much taxes your energy.

Holding Back Negative Feelings

In my personal and clinical experience, I've found that when people hold back strong negative feelings, they end up expressing those feelings in roundabout ways. For example, let's say you disapprove of your stepson's treatment of his friends but saying anything seems to aggravate the situation. It will be important for you to find a way to handle your negative feelings, or else you may pull back and close your heart to your relationship with your stepson.

Techniques for Coping with Strong Negative Emotions

- Be aware that you have them.
- Accept them.
- Try to understand where they come from and, if need be, seek support.

Our feelings are not the problem; it's pushing our feelings down inside us until they get stuck that creates symptoms (such as anxiety, depression, and anger). Letting yourself air your emotions can help you keep your balance. Talking with a close friend, family member, spouse, minister, or counselor can give some release and an opportunity to sort out the jumble of feelings you are experiencing.

Feelings tend to ebb and flow like the tides, and it's best not to react too strongly to them. You can use your feelings to help guide your decisions, but be aware that feelings are temporary; they tend to change just as the winds and tides of the ocean are always changing. If you want to take some action because of negative feelings that you are having, it is much better to wait until you are in a calm state before acting.

Many family squabbles come from wishing that people or situations would be different than they are. This desire, coupled with constructive action, is often the impetus for positive change to occur. Simply wishing out loud that a situation or person is different than it is doesn't usually change anything except to create tension, conflict, and feelings of rejection in the other person. When you accept the reality of each moment, you are in a better place from which to find solutions and make decisions.

Everyone Gets Angry Sometimes

Even the Dalai Lama admits to getting angry sometimes. He says that he allows himself to feel the anger in the moment that it occurs but doesn't remain attached to that moment or that anger. In each new moment, he lets go of the feeling from the last moment. Meditation is a great tool for calming the mind; people who practice some kind of peaceful contemplation on a regular basis find themselves better able to handle upsets when they occur. For some of us, sitting meditation is too difficult. There are many ways to find quiet repose that can help us to heal the mind and gain perspective over emotions. Some people find their meditation through silent walking, prayer, various types of martial arts, music, or yoga.

Psychological Symptoms of Stress
- Anger, irritability, moodiness, and low tolerance for frustration
- Self-doubt and low self-esteem
- Feelings of grief and loss
- Feelings of inadequacy, helplessness, shame, guilt, and misunderstanding
- Mental or emotional fatigue
- A cynical and pessimistic attitude

Some Suggestions for Managing Stress
- Take responsibility for your feelings, and don't blame them on other people.
- Try not to hold on to negative stories of the ex-spouse or any other people.
- Cultivate awareness of your thoughts (mindfulness) and take charge of your thoughts.
- Reprogram yourself to look for the positive in everything.
- Take a minimum of five to ten minutes a day to be in nature or meditate (activate the relaxation response).

- Exercise thirty minutes a day.
- Get enough sleep (at least seven hours a night).
- Eat healthy food and drink plenty of water.
- Surround yourself with positive people. Both happiness and depression are contagious.
- Take charge of your thoughts.
- Seize the day.
- Seek laughter.

EXERCISES TO INCREASE YOUR UNDERSTANDING AND AWARENESS

1. What are some of your stress buttons?

_____

_____

_____

_____

2. What is the best way to handle yourself when your buttons get pushed? Write it down and then check to see if your spouse agrees with your answer.

_____

_____

_____

_____

_____

_____

3. How do your stepkids respond to stress?

_____

_____

_____

_____

_____

_____

4. What can you do to help them when they are stressed? (If you don't know, you can always ask them.)

_____

_____

_____

_____

_____

_____

5. Find a comfortable and quiet place to sit. Close your eyes and quiet your mind. Just notice your breath. If thoughts come into your mind and you realize that you are thinking, gently bring yourself back to noticing your breath. Do this for a minimum of five minutes a day.

6. Do the same exercise as #5 but pick a single word and keep your mind on that word. It should be a neutral word like *one* or *tree.*

7. Put one hand on your chest and one hand on your lower belly. Breathe deeply and see which moves more—your chest or your lower belly. Keep taking deep breaths and try to get your lower belly to extend more than your chest when you are inhaling. When you breathe deep into your lower belly like this, you are expanding your lungs and bringing more oxygen into your body, which is relaxing, cleansing, and energizing

Chapter Six

Know Thyself

"One's dignity is measured, not by one's past,
but by one's present actions."
—Thanissaro Bhikkhu,
American Buddhist monk

"My dad told me that you are a bad man," little Tommy said to his stepfather Mikel. Tommy seemed nervous and uncertain. "Daddy said that you have done bad things."

Mikel took a deep breath and knelt down so that he was at Tommy's level. "I'm not going to lie to you, kiddo," Mikel said as he looked into Tommy's keen green eyes. "I have made my share of mistakes in this life. But I think that I've learned from them."

Mikel had had a drinking problem. His own father was an alcoholic, as were his grandfather and his great-grandfather. During his first marriage, he had been arrested for domestic violence. He also had been arrested twice for driving while under the influence of alcohol. Since those troubled years, Mikel had become a twelve-stepper and sobered up. Counseling in conjunction with mandatory anger management classes had helped him to turn things around for himself. But it had come too late to save his first marriage.

Mikel met Tommy's mother in the Alcoholics Anonymous program. They were friends for about a year before they started dating. Tommy's father had not wanted the divorce from Tommy's mother. And he resented that Tommy now had another man in his life. He made no bones about it; he wanted to alienate Tommy from his stepfather because he didn't want to be replaced.

Mikel sat the ten-year-old boy down. "Tommy," he said, "I have a drinking problem. It's almost like I'm allergic to alcohol. I can't drink like a regular person. When I drink alcohol, I'm much more likely to make mistakes like I did in the past. I wasn't nice to my wife and I did stupid, dangerous things like drive when I was drunk. But you don't need to worry about it, Tommy, because I don't drink anymore. I haven't had a drink in more than five years now. And I don't plan on having one ever again."

"But my Daddy said that I shouldn't trust you." Tommy looked skeptically into Mikel's eyes. "How do I know that you won't be mean to my mommy or me?"

"The only way you'll know is over time, Tommy. I understand. I'm going to have to earn your trust." Mikel patted his shoulder gently. "Your dad is just looking out for you. He loves you and doesn't want anything bad to happen to you. That's what dads are supposed to do—protect their kids. And I'm your stepdaddy. I want to protect you, too. But first I have to earn your trust. You and your dad are just going to have to wait and see that I have changed. It will take some time for both of you to trust me. Okay?"

"Okay," said Tommy with a small smile.

"And Tommy?" Mikel added. "Your dad and I hardly ever see each other. After you've been around me for a while, you'll have to decide for yourself." He gently patted his shoulder again. "But there's no hurry. You just take your time to feel comfortable. I'm not going anywhere." And with that, Mikel got up and turned to Tommy's mother, his new wife, and said, "I'm going to take a walk. Be back in about twenty minutes, everyone."

"There is no power in the universe, nor any form of intercession that can separate a cause from its effect, action from reaction, or a man from consequences for his deeds."
—TALBOT MUNDY

The way we behave now creates our future experiences. If we don't like the way things are going in our lives, we can change direction at any time—just as Mikel apparently has done in his life. In this example, he takes responsibility for his past and his present, determined to prove himself trustworthy in the days to come. When we learn from our experiences and don't blame others for what "happens" to us, everything becomes an opportunity to grow and refine our character. With awareness and practical application, we can actually transform some of our relationships and atmosphere. Mikel isn't defensive with Tommy; he doesn't try to argue him out of what he is feeling or has heard. He kindly reassures him in such a way that Tommy senses that Mikel is not going to hurt him.

When we are clear on our purpose and intention (in this example, Mikel wants to have a positive relationship with Tommy), we can choose our behaviors more thoughtfully and wisely. For example, the more we practice kindness, the more we will experience the benefits of that choice, and the more it will reflect back to us. Do your best to respond with kindness to your stepchildren—even if it doesn't warm their hearts in the moment, you are doing several things. You are behaving in a way that you can feel good about and that actually is good for your health. And your kindness will most likely be reflected back to you at another time—by your stepchildren, other members of their family, or other people who love them.

Did You Know?
- When we do an act of kindness, it enhances our immune system.
- When we observe an act of kindness, it enhances our immune system.
- When we receive an act of kindness, it enhances our immune system.

For more than seven years, Ed's ex-wife tormented him and his new wife, Joanne. She created drama and problems for them at every turn. Their son Ricky was stuck in the middle of the ongoing war between his parents. Ricky's mom was quite disturbed, and she used her son to spy on his stepmom and dad. He would call his mom from their house and tell her about their every move. He would go through their drawers and tell his mother about the personal items he found, which she would use to embarrass them. Ricky ignored his stepmom most of the time and refused to treat her respectfully, although Joanne was very decent toward Ricky. She took care of him as she would have her own child, even though she had no control over the way he was being raised. His father was driven by a desire to avoid conflict with his ex-wife because she was so difficult. Joanne forced herself to be kind toward Ricky even though her anger and resentment would build and burst out in fights with Ed from time to time. Joanne always kept in mind that Ricky was in a terrible position. She saw him as virtually brainwashed by his mom and hoped that someday he would emerge from her toxic influence. When she was feeling hurt or upset, she kept her distance from Ricky. She never reacted in a hostile way or took her anger out on Ricky.

Eventually, Joanne and Ed sought counseling; they learned to manage the situation so that Ed's ex-wife didn't create as much havoc in their lives. Ed made a point to minimize his contact with his ex-wife, keeping to email as much as possible. When she sent a ranting or toxic email filled with nonsensical accusations (such as "I know you are using drugs over there," or "I know that you are trying to turn my friends against me and that is why they won't call me back," or "You are a terrible father who doesn't care about his son"), Ed disciplined himself to not respond, even though he would have liked to. When Ricky turned fifteen, he started warming up to his dad and stepmom, and eventually he grew to appreciate how decent Joanne had been to him. She never uttered a negative word about his mother. She focused on trying to do the right thing out of her own integrity, love for her husband, and caring for her stepson.

Joanne worked hard to not take things personally—she created lots of support and meaning in her life through other avenues.

Practicing loving detachment can be helpful for weathering any rejection or ambivalence that you receive from your stepchildren. Ricky had been hearing for years about what a terrible person Joanne was. But Joanne held her ground and tried hard to do the right thing. Eventually, Ricky's direct experiences with Joanne trumped what he had been told by his mom. Once he started trusting his own feelings about Joanne—as opposed to simply accepting his mom's view—he was also able to start developing his own independent perspective on other aspects of his life.

Mindfulness, Acceptance, and Unresolved Emotional Issues

Being a stepparent is bound to kick up unresolved emotional issues that you've been carrying around for a while. If you pay attention, you'll notice that the same issues keep coming up. It may be a series of uncomfortable thoughts that keep giving you the same feeling. Let's use an example of a stepfather who grew up as an only child of a poor, single mother. In grade school, Michael had holes in his shoes and baggy hand-me-downs from his older cousins. He was shy and ostracized by his classmates. He was the last one picked when they selected sports teams. Even though he is now all grown up and very successful, he is terribly insecure. Growing up, he'd felt ashamed of their poverty and not having a father around. He'd felt abandoned and "less than." These are important factors that can deeply affect our psychology and then influence our attitudes and behaviors. It became very important to Michael that his children and stepchildren have the best of everything. He thought that in this way he was showing them love and keeping them from having any of the painful experiences that he had. Some of his children appreciated his generosity, but others resented it. They felt that it came with strings—that their father was more interested in how they looked and what they had than who they were. They grew tired of his stories retelling his childhood challenges and began rolling their eyes when he launched into one. Michael would then get angry and feel unappreciated; his deeply rooted confusion about who he really was became triggered. Unless he comes to understand where these reactions within him are coming from, he will continue to be frustrated, going around and around on the merry-go-round.

So when you notice that the same old feelings keep getting kicked up in your experiences with your family, it can become an opportunity to look within and reevaluate what your true intentions are behind your behaviors. Are they really for you, or for others? Are you trying to heal some old wounds? Are your actions, attitudes, and thought patterns an effort to avoid or repair some aspect of your psyche? Is it working? Being a stepparent offers an excellent opportunity to increase your insight and discernment about who and how you really want to be in the world.

Points to Ponder

- Try to be aware of your thinking patterns.
- Notice what triggers certain feelings inside you.
- Try to use your awareness to intentionally redirect your focus; for example, when you find you are reacting in a particular negative pattern, step back and assess whether the situation is triggering some underlying issue that you have. When this happens, it can color your perspective and make things assume more importance than they actually merit.
- The more unaware you are about your own issues, the more power they have over you. Even if you are justified in your upset about something, when you are aware that old buttons are also being pushed, it can help your evaluation of the situation to be more accurate.
- When thinking about your stepchildren and their intentions toward you, pay special attention to and notice any gestures of acceptance and appreciation from them.

As a stepparents, those of us who have the tendency to anticipate rejection or negative judgment from others won't have far to look. When we have these mental messages coming from unconscious belief systems in our own minds, we look for cues to confirm our fears. Obviously, if you look for signs of unfair treatment or rejection from your stepkids, chances are you will find them.

When you are calm and aware, in the here and now, rather than the "there" and "then," it can allow you to step out of your same old pattern of emotional reactivity. Learning to observe without judgment the feelings and thoughts that you are having can help slow down your reaction time; this can help you to cultivate more mature ways of responding in difficult moments. Certainly, problems will arise in the present moment that you may feel the need to address. But as soon as possible, try to fill the present moment with thoughts, awareness, and actions that promote feelings of happiness, peace, and calm.

All major world religions advocate the same six virtues for how to live a good life:[5]

- Wisdom
- Courage
- Justice
- Humanity
- Temperance
- Transcendence

Researchers Martin Seligman, PhD, and Chris Peterson, PhD, discovered twenty-four character strengths that were identified within these virtues. To find out what your top character strengths are, you can go to www.authentichappiness.com and take the VIA Survey of Character Strengths. There is also a VIA Strength Survey for Children. It can be fun as a family to learn each member's top character strengths and help each other cultivate these.

---

5 Christopher Peterson and Martin E. P. Seligman, *Character Strengths and Virtues: A Handbook and Classification* (New York: Oxford University Press and Washington, DC: American Psychological Association, 2004).

- Once you've identified your strengths, find ways to use them in your daily life.
- Find ways to help your loved ones use theirs.
- Apply your character strengths to your life every day to improve your happiness and relationships.

EXERCISES

1. Write down five of your strongest character strengths. Here are some examples of character strengths: curiosity, courage, enthusiasm and zest, appreciation of beauty, love, perseverance, industry, love of learning, wisdom, creativity, gratitude. If you like, you can go to the website www.authentichappiness.com and take the VIA survey, which will tell you what your top five character strengths are. It only takes about fifteen minutes. You will also find other interesting assessments to test for happiness level, depression, and optimism. List your top five strengths from the survey or choose on your own.

_____

_____

_____

_____

_____

_____

2. Write about how you are practicing these strengths in your family and how you might apply them each day.

_____

_____

_____

_____

_____

_____

_____

_____

Chapter Seven

The Power of Perseverance

*"We can only change our selves and not others.
We must be the change we want to see."*
—GANDHI

Ellen and Allan started their relationship while Allan was still married. Allan eventually left his wife to be with Ellen. Allan's ex-wife Rolli made it clear to their ten-year-old daughter Gracie that her father had cheated. Naturally, this put Gracie in a very challenging situation, especially when she spent time with her father and stepmother. Not only was Gracie hurt and angry—but she thought it was her duty to honor her mother by rejecting her stepmother. It's easy to understand how Gracie might feel confused and angry in the situation.

At first, Ellen tried to be patient with Gracie's rejection of her. She felt guilty about having started her relationship as an affair with a married man and accepted Gracie's relentless negativity toward her. Over time, out of self-protection, Ellen distanced herself from Gracie. She felt hurt and developed a subtle hostile undertone in her attitude toward Gracie. Ellen felt entitled to her resentment toward Gracie.

It was easier for Gracie to forgive her father than her stepmother. So while Allan and Gracie were able to repair their father-daughter relationship, the negativity between Ellen and Gracie wore away at the marriage. Allan and Ellen had long talks about taking responsibility for the predicament that they'd created for Gracie. They agreed that while they would not accept disrespectful or abusive treatment from Gracie, whenever possible Ellen would do her best to be kind and gentle toward her stepdaughter. Ellen took responsibility for her choices and tried to be understanding of Gracie's hurt and anger. She tried to find the delicate balance of having compassion and forgiveness toward Gracie without tolerating abusive behavior. Allan tried to be supportive and loving to both his new wife and daughter, while insisting that his daughter behave respectfully toward her stepmother. Gracie continued to keep her distance from Ellen; eventually they forged a neutral, nonadversarial relationship. Eventually, Allan's ex-wife Rolli met someone and moved forward with her life. Gracie's parents were happier than she'd seen them before. It took about six years, but Gracie came to accept Allan and Ellen as a couple. When Gracie was an adult struggling with her own romantic relationships, she developed more appreciation for how it takes two to tango. Even though she did not agree with her stepmother having had a relationship with her father when he was still married to her mother, she was grateful that in retrospect, Ellen had been forgiving of how much Gracie had rejected her.

In moments of contention, biological parents sometimes tell their new spouses that their children from a previous marriage are their own responsibility. Although stepparents may take a secondary role in raising the biological children of a spouse, the way they relate to their stepchildren can significantly impact the family dynamics. Sometimes, a stepparent's role may be to offer a more objective view of the family's daily life. After divorce, many parents go easy on disciplining their children because they are preoccupied with putting their lives back together or they feel concerned about causing the children additional stress. Ideally, stepparents can communicate their opinions about situations with the children, directly and diplomatically, without blame or criticism.

Points to Ponder
- Offering your thoughts is different than telling your partner what to do!
- Model the behavior you would like to teach.

The Role of Stepparents
- We need to put our ego aside a lot.
- We must commit ourselves to supporting and loving our stepchildren.
- We must assist the children in standing on their own two feet and making their individual ways in the world.

Loyalty Conflicts
- Don't speak negatively about your partner's ex-spouse in front of your stepchildren.
- Children share their parents' DNA; their self-esteem can suffer when their parents are chronically criticized.
- Kids may feel the need to take sides, and it's not likely to be yours.
- Find a way to cope with or change the situation so that your feelings don't spill over on the children.
- Get support from your spouse, a friend, or a counselor when you need it.

Walter was a military man and the single dad of an adopted son, Max. When Walter married, Max was eight years old and Stephanie's daughter Destiny was ten. It was a tough adjustment for Destiny because her mom and dad didn't require much of her, while Walter had strong beliefs about kids needing to participate in the household by doing chores.

At first, Stephanie allowed Walter to set the rules. She asked Destiny to cooperate because they had moved into Walter's house.

Destiny complied but complained bitterly to her father about how things were at her mother's house. Eventually, Destiny's father complained to Stephanie about the rigid, military-style environment at Walter's house. Stephanie had also grown uncomfortable with the extreme nature of the chores and rules. The complaints from her ex-husband gave her the courage to speak up.

Needless to say, Walter was not pleased with Stephanie's newfound assertiveness. They began having heated arguments, which the children overheard. Destiny grew more resentful toward Walter, and Max withdrew from the family. Alarmed that they could not seem to find a middle ground, Walter and Stephanie sought counseling. They were aware that the fabric of their marriage had begun to fray.

After they tired of arguing about who was right and wrong, they started talking about what the issues meant to them. Walter's mother had died when he was a young boy, and his father, who held a high rank in the military and moved a lot, didn't feel that he could care for Walter. Walter's paternal grandmother raised him according to his father's instructions. His father had strict guidelines and requirements that Walter help his grandmother around the house. The only accolades that Walter experienced from his father came when he toed the line accordingly.

The only way that Walter knew how to love children was by being a strict taskmaster. When Stephanie argued with him about it, he felt disrespected because no one ever argued with his father. Getting beneath the surface allowed Stephanie to see Walter's vulnerability—that it wasn't as much a control issue as it was Walter parenting in the only way he knew how.

Stephanie became tearful when she heard Walter's story and thanked him for trying to be a good stepfather to Destiny. She cried and told him how much she loved him. She expressed her fear that they were losing their family; that this method wasn't going to work for them. Destiny had been raised differently and she was feeling alienated in her mother's new home, which broke her mother's heart. Stephanie felt like she was compromising her daughter's well-being for her own happiness and was questioning whether she should remain in the marriage. However, once they learned in counseling how to understand each other at a deeper level, they found it easier to compromise.

Eventually, they brought the children into a family counseling session and together they decided what each child's chores would be, and the consequences for not doing the assigned work. The children felt good about being part of the process. Max felt liberated by being given a voice, and Destiny agreed that it was good for her to have some chores. Stephanie and Walter both felt less alone, more like partners. They grew closer. Walter was able to stretch outside of his comfort zone and was rewarded with more closeness and love. Stephanie was more assertive, which brought her respect and responsiveness from her husband.

Points to Ponder

- Stepparents should at first establish a relationship with the children akin to being a friend or "camp counselor," rather than a disciplinarian.
- Children can benefit when they are involved in creating the rules and expectations in the household.
- It works better when household rules are enforced by the biological parent—until the stepparent and children develop a solid bond.

Taking Responsibility for Our Mistakes

David and Joni were eleven and thirteen years old when their parents divorced. Their father Al remarried a woman named Doris about a year later. Three months after the wedding, David and Joni's mother was hospitalized with severe mental illness. The kids were taken to visit their mom at the hospital, but it was very distressing to them. When she was released from the hospital, she didn't continue treatment or medication, and descended into a downward spiral of mental illness and alcoholism. The children didn't see their mom for years.

Doris did her best to pick up the slack. The responsibility was more than she'd bargained for, as they now had the children full-time with their mother out of the picture for the time being. But Doris had always wanted children, so she tried to rise to the occasion.

Unfortunately, the children were not as receptive as she would have liked. She would make them their favorite meal, and they would suddenly lose their appetites. She would try to cuddle them and offer them comfort; sometimes they would let her, and other times they would push her away. The kids were anxious about their mother and ambivalent about her "replacement."

After fifteen months of devoted service, Doris ran out of steam. She felt hurt and unappreciated by the kids and her husband. Doris tended to just the basics and taught David and Joni to be as self-reliant as possible. She believed that was the best option at the time. As teenagers, she insisted they get jobs and buy their own clothes. This in itself was not a problem, except that Doris and Al had adopted three-year-old Lacy when Al's children were in their early teens. David and Joni saw a difference between how their younger sibling was raised and treated by their parents. It was obvious to them that Doris loved her adopted daughter Lacy differently than her stepchildren. She doted on Lacy and spoiled her, and Al followed his wife's lead. Al was a passive fellow and insensitive to the way his children felt about it.

When Joni was an adult she moved clear across the country and distanced herself from her family. David started a family of his own and stayed local. After he had his own children (and watched as the indulgence of his younger stepsister continued into her adulthood), David realized he was angry about the inequities. He tried to talk with his stepmother and father about the feelings that he had about his childhood.

Doris and Al both vehemently denied that the children had been raised any differently. They became indignant when David even mentioned the idea, and questioned his purpose in bringing this up. David only wanted them to acknowledge his experience and perhaps even apologize. He told them he understood that it would have been easier to love an adopted child, who presented fewer complications. In truth, he loved his parents and appreciated Doris as the person who had cared the most for him as a child. After he told them of his concerns, a rift developed between David and his parents, who could not acknowledge having made any mistakes or doing anything less than perfectly.

Making Mistakes
- Making mistakes is natural.
- A mistake can create an opportunity for problem solving and reconciliation.
- Mending mistakes can result in feelings of greater closeness and commitment to the relationship or family.

Time Frames
- Stepfamilies starting with young children may have an easier time than those formed with adolescent children, due to the differing developmental stages.
- Children ten to fourteen years old may have the most difficult time adjusting to a stepfamily.
- Children fifteen years old and older are naturally more interested in developing their individualism rather than putting a lot of investment in stepfamily life.
- Children under age ten are usually more accepting of a new adult in the family, particularly when the adult is a positive influence.

Household Rules
A couple in California found a great solution to the potential pitfalls of forming a blended family. Santiago and Sofia each brought two children to the marriage, which was the second for both of them. Sofia stayed home with their children while Santiago worked outside of the home. They spent a year working on a shared framework for disciplining the children; both agreed that they would discipline their own biological children. When one partner

spends more time at home with the children than the other, it can pose a problem in dealing with issues that arise while he is at work. In this California couple's case, Santiago was exceptionally consistent and clear with his children regarding what was expected of them, as well as the consequences if they were to misbehave. After discussing the ground rules with the kids, the parents asked them to help determine their own punishments for breaking the rules. This stepmother told me that when her stepchildren needed disciplining and their father was away, she would say to them, "What do you think your father would say about this?"

The kids would usually say, "He wouldn't like it."

Sofia would then say, "What do you think your father would say that you should do now?"

"He would say that we should take a time out," the children would reply.

It was that simple. This stepmother was being sensitive to her stepchildren's feelings and not attempting to discipline them herself, but she was helping them as an "older friend" and authority figure in their shared household. She was also acting in a supportive capacity to her husband, their father. This was an ideal arrangement created by this couple through careful deliberation and practice. It allowed the stepmom to be an active participant in raising the children, while being sensitive to their preference to be disciplined by their biological parent.

After the Divorce

After a divorce, children usually adjust better when they have regular and consistent time with both of their parents. Once parents remarry, fathers especially often spend less time with their children. On average, dads decrease their visits with their children by half within the first year of remarriage. The less a parent visits, the more a child is likely to feel abandoned. Nonresidential parents can connect with their children by developing special activities that they both enjoy. Stepparents can encourage one-on-one time and blended family time with the children.

Tips for Adults in the Blended Family

- Don't disagree in front of the children—decide in private.
- Practice patience—don't lose your temper.
- Make the well-being of the children a top priority.
- Remember that the children benefit from the model of a happy relationship.
- Model kindness and forgiveness (most likely you'll have ample opportunities).
- Develop new traditions and rituals while respecting first-family ones. (Examples: A gratitude exercise at dinner where everyone goes around the table and says something that they are grateful for that happened that day or tells about something positive that happened that day.)

EXERCISES

1. What do you think that your role in your family is?

_____

_____

_____

_____

_____

_____

2. How satisfied are you with your relationships with your stepchildren, your spouse, and the extended blended family?

_____

_____

_____

_____

_____

_____

3. What can you do to improve these relationships?

Action item one: _____

Action item two: _____

Action item three: _____

For example, "I can create a safe, loving, nonjudgmental environment as much as possible," or "I can let my stepchildren know that I respect their opinions when expressed in a respectful manner."

Chapter Eight

Advice from Stepkids

"To be interested in the changing seasons is a happier state of mind than to be hopelessly in love with spring."
—GEORGE SANTAYANA

Fifty stepchildren of different ages were asked to give advice to stepparents, and this is a summary of what they said:

- "Don't try to replace the mother or father."
- "Be a friend. Don't try to be their parent."
- "Try hard not to take things personally."
- "Remember that you are the grown up, they are the kid. Behave accordingly."
- "You chose to have stepchildren; they didn't choose to have a stepparent."
- "Be patient."
- "If you can, try to love your stepkids as if they were your own."
- "Don't love them as if they were your own children."
- "Don't push your relationship with them."
- "If my brother and I still secretly wish my dad and mom would get back together, don't take it personally. It's not about you."

- "Blended families are like organ transplants; sometimes they take and sometimes they don't."
- "Never talk about the parent that you are not married to as a way of making conversation with your stepkids. It makes everyone feel awkward."
- "Don't try to change the parenting style of the original parents."
- "If your stepkids don't want to talk, don't make them talk. Give them space. Give them a day. If it continues longer, then you can ask if there is something wrong—but if they still don't want to talk about it, go tell their parent, your spouse, that something seems to be bothering the child."
- "Don't feel badly if they don't want to eat your food."
- "Don't open their door without knocking. Wait for them to say 'come in' before opening the door."

More Suggestions

- Contrary to popular myth, love takes time to develop. Give your relationships with your stepchildren time to grow and develop naturally. Forcing closeness is often ineffective. Sometimes, it may even damage your relationship. Encourage the children to call you by your given name to avoid confusion and conflict about parenting roles.
- Set aside some one-on-one time for each of your children and stepchildren, and respect their individual needs and wants. If your children or stepchildren want to vent their feelings about the divorce or remarriage, listen openly and validate their feelings without agreeing with them. For example, "I can understand how you'd feel that way" vs. "Yes, I agree [or I feel] the same way." Be patient as they deal with the loss of their original family structure; some people take years to recover.
- Keep in mind the challenges of raising children between two households. Although it's ideal to strive for as much consistency between households as possible, often you'll need to accept and be respectful of the differences. Encourage your children and stepchildren to maintain control over their own

clothes and other personal items—even if they have to share closets or bedrooms. Keep the children's teachers informed of family changes that may affect their social behavior or school performance.

- Strengthen your parenting relationship with your partner. Discuss parenting roles, beliefs, and expectations. It may help to take a parenting class or to work with a counselor.
- Develop simple, explicit rules for your children to follow. In most cases, it's often best for each parent to be the primary disciplinarian for his or her own children, with the stepparent filling in for emergencies and gradually taking on the role of an emerging parent. Remember, parents are most effective when they provide a unified front. Instead of responding immediately to a child's request, confer with your spouse and make a mutual decision.
- If the kids have family pictures that include both of their parents, let them display the pictures. Don't let your insecurities get in the way of the kids wanting to have pictures in their own room at your house.

Pacing Your Stepkids

About a year after her father had remarried, twelve-year-old Susie went through a brief period of insomnia. Her stepmother Audrey often got up with her in the middle of the night to comfort her, rub her back, and help her get back to sleep. Audrey had four grown biological daughters of her own and was very experienced with soothing little girls.

One night when Audrey was gently massaging Susie during the middle of the night, their connection felt especially good—until Susie turned to Audrey and said, "If I need someone to be with me, my mom is always going to be my first choice. And my dad will be my second choice. If neither of them is available, then I'll want another adult person. But my mom will always be my first choice." Audrey told her that she understood. Then she asked Susie what her ideal relationship with her stepparents would look like.

Susie said she would be fine if, when she walked into the house, her stepparents said "hey" and she replied "hey," and then they both did their own thing. Susie told Audrey that she felt pressured to say, "I love you," back to her and that she didn't need to be told over and again how happy Audrey was that Susie was at their house.

Audrey felt hurt and rejected; after all, she had only been trying to make Susie feel welcome and loved. But she tried not to take it personally. She knew that as a stepparent, she needed to be sensitive to her stepdaughter's readiness to establish a close relationship. She decided Susie's reaction was less about her feelings for Audrey, and more about Susie's natural process of becoming comfortable with her blended family.

From that day on, Audrey kept a friendly distance. When Susie came over, Audrey would just say hello and go about her business. She was kind and decent toward Susie but remained somewhat detached. The detachment helped her cope with her hurt feelings and also prevented any spontaneous demonstrations of love that might fly out of her mouth or heart. Inspired by her love for Susie, she worked on self-regulation in order to respect Susie's wishes. Children of parents who are good at self-regulation are happier. Audrey reported that Susie seemed to notice the change. Audrey gave Susie more space without hostility—kindly respecting what Susie had requested. Susie was startled by the difference in Audrey at first, and then she realized Audrey was responding to their middle-of-the-night conversation. Most fourteen-year-olds are a little fickle and maybe even disoriented. Their hormones, bodies, and social environment are changing faster than they can keep up with. Kids at this age especially need room to stretch and fluctuate in their feelings. Once Audrey backed off, Susie started approaching Audrey. She began going up to Audrey when she arrived for her stay and giving her a hug. She started asking her to play chess with her, or confiding in Audrey with intimate details about her life. Once Audrey accepted Susie as she was, without the pressure to relate, she began to seek out a relationship with Audrey. She became more open to loving and being loved. Audrey became extremely conscientious about not pushing her love on her stepdaughter.

Everyone has different needs that change all the time. As Audrey stopped trying so hard to be the perfect stepmother, her relationship with Susie became more relaxed and natural. All parents need to delicately ride out the fluctuating tide of adolescence, but stepparents have to be especially careful to respect the emotional boundaries set by their children.

Children can inspire us to stretch our capacity to love and then extend our hearts into the world. Many stepparents are eager to have a relationship with their stepchildren, but the kids may have different ideas. It can take anywhere from two to seven years for blended families to integrate, and for children to develop strong bonds with their stepparents. Yours may be quicker or even slower. It's hard to not take this personally, but it's critical to pace the children's readiness for a relationship. Try to spend time together, whether it is watching a movie, or sharing a meal or an adventure; creating good memories together helps to weave the fabric of a sturdy relationship.

For example, Fred had been teased and bullied by his peers and brothers when he was a kid. His sixteen-year-old stepson Jake ignored him most of the time. Fred offered him respectful greetings, but Jake felt conflicted with his loyalty toward his father. For Fred, it was hard not to take it personally. His automatic reaction was to feel rejected and depressed and to withdraw from the relationship. It brought back old ghosts to haunt him—feeling hurt and weak as a kid. Sometimes he felt angry toward Jake. Fred understood where his feelings came from, and he tried to see things from Jake's point of view. He made an effort to go to Jake's soccer matches to show his interest and looked for opportunities to build their relationship slowly over time. Fred accepted Jake and while he expected to be treated with the decency that should be afforded a stranger, he recognized that he had to earn Jake's respect and friendship. He lowered his expectation for the relationship. Over time, Fred and

Jake developed a friendship that was based on their own history and Fred's consistent attitude of caring.

Teenagers usually run hot and cold with their biological parents. Biological parents often get moments of warm connection with their children that stepparents may not receive. While coping with rejection from an adolescent, it helps if you don't take him or her too personally. Remember, they are in a stage of self-discovery and independence. The last thing most teenagers want is to have to bond with another "parental unit." This is a normal part of their developmental process.

Hang in There

Elliot and Barry were stepbrothers who didn't get along. When their parents got married they were both thirteen years old. There were several other children in the household and not enough bedrooms for everyone. Elliot and Barry were the most natural choice to share a bedroom because they were the same age, but they were opposites in every way and they drove each other crazy. Their conflicts bled over to their parents—who of course each sided with his or her own child and found fault with the stepchild. The parents worried that they had made a mistake having the boys share a room, but they didn't have any better solutions. Within a year, their oldest child left for college, freeing up a bedroom so the boys could have their own rooms. The atmosphere in the house then mellowed, and all was forgotten as the conflicts faded away. Today, at the age of twenty-two, the boys are the best of friends, and they consider themselves brothers.

EXERCISES

1. Before you got married, what did you imagine that being a stepparent would be like?

_____

_____

_____

_____

_____

_____

_____

_____

2. How is it different than what you thought it would be?

_____

_____

_____

_____

_____

_____

_____

_____

_____

3. Find a quiet moment to ask your stepkids how your relationship is going from their perspective. Is there anything that they would like to change, or is there anything in particular that they especially like about it? Ask your spouse how he/she feels about your current relationship with the kids.

Chapter Nine

Creating a Better Reality

"Only through our connectedness to others can we really know and enhance the self; and only through working on the self can we begin to enhance our connectedness to others."
—HARRIET LERNER

Bob bought tickets to a baseball game, planning to take his twin stepsons. When he asked them to go, they said that they weren't that interested in seeing the game. Then some friends of theirs invited them to go the same game, and they agreed to go. Bob became very upset and complained bitterly to his wife Isabella that no matter how hard he tried, his stepsons continued to reject him. As usual, she told him that he shouldn't take it personally; the boys just wanted to be with their friends. Isabella reassured him that in time, they would come around.

Bob had been an only child of parents with severe alcohol problems and radical mood swings. As a boy, he felt that if only he were more loveable or even likeable, then his parents would be nicer to him. As an adult, he grew to understand that it hadn't been his fault as a kid. But deep down, he was still conditioned by his childhood and alert for people to be unpredictably angry or standoffish when he least expected it. So, when his stepsons rebuffed his overtures of friendship, his feelings of rejection were painful.

Bob wanted Isabella to take some action with the boys—to let them know that they were hurting their stepfather's feelings. He wanted her to tell them to be more open to him. She tried, but he never felt it was enough. The boys felt imposed upon.

"He's your husband, Mom. We want to be with our friends or Dad. We barely even know him."

Their mom would ask, "Well, how are you going to ever get to know him if you don't spend time with him?"

And so it went for years. Sometimes Bob was so disappointed that he withdrew from his marriage into a cocoon of self-pity. He realized that he didn't have any control over his stepsons or their interest in having a relationship with him. Eventually, he recognized that his wife didn't either. To make matters worse, his old patterns of thinking and reacting were getting in the way of his marriage.

As a stepparent, I've found that the complex, previously uncharted relationships within my blended family have inspired me to reprogram my own ways of responding to the world around me. The way we think and what we believe affects how we behave and feel. And we tend to create the relationships and lives that we think and believe we can have. If I want to focus on my sixteen-year-old stepdaughter's not wanting to go shopping with me and feel rejected, I can. Alternatively, if I think about the good feelings created when we all had lunch together, my heart is filled with warmth and promise. I have the power to focus on a positive moment, even an exchanged smile, which recharges my energy toward relationship building.

When you are having a problem with any member of your stepfamily, first consider if you are contributing to the problem. Something about your perspective or behavior could be exacerbating the situation. In every relationship, there is a dance of sorts, and we all have our steps. Most of us have reflexive negative reactions based on conditioning experiences in our past. These patterns may have developed as a way of protecting ourselves in previous situations but can hinder us in the present day.

Points to Ponder

- If we think negatively about our stepchildren or their biological parents, they feel it—subconsciously or consciously.
- Even if you don't speak your negative thoughts, they have an effect.
- As human beings, we actually have the ability to choose our thoughts; we can choose to focus on more positive aspects about our situation and family members.
- If a stepparent sends out kind, peaceful, accepting, no-pressure vibes, stepchildren and other family members are more likely to respond to them in kind.

EXERCISE

Write down some of your own negative tendencies or responses that are being triggered in your experience as a stepparent.

_____

_____

_____

_____

_____

_____

_____

_____

_____

_____

_____

Missing the Moment

When Rachel's husband tucked his kids into bed at night, they would ask for Rachel to come too. Rachel refused because she thought it was too indulgent for both parents do a one-person job.

She didn't mention it to them, but she felt uncomfortable in this touchy-feely arena.

Rachel started therapy because she felt alienated in her stepfamily. She thought her husband should be stricter with the kids because that's how she was raised. Her parents were emotionally reserved, puritanical folks. They believed in right and wrong with little to no gray in between.

When Rachel was a child, her parents had no tolerance of any opposition to or even questioning of the rules. No one ever seemed to care how she felt. In order to cooperate and get along, she went numb and did what was required of her. There wasn't much warmth or connectedness in Rachel's childhood home, so her trust in loving relationships was tentative. When it came to her stepchildren, any hiccup could set her confidence backward. She kept her stepkids at arm's length as a self-protective mechanism.

So when Rachel's stepchildren asked to be tucked in by both parents, she insisted on kissing them goodnight downstairs and having their father tuck them in alone. Amazingly, they continued asking her to tuck them in until they were teenagers. Rachel had missed an opportunity to bond with her stepchildren. She rejected their request for closeness out of her own stringent beliefs and fears.

When Rachel came for therapy, she had little awareness of the unconscious belief system she had developed as a child. Eventually, when she became more aware of what was happening in her own mind, she was able to rethink her perspective. As Rachel slowly freed herself from her old constricting beliefs, she felt a renewed energy. In time, she opened her heart more to her husband and her stepchildren. They in turn became more available for a reciprocal loving connection.

EXERCISES:

Are there unconscious beliefs and fears that are holding you back in some way from loving as fully as you can?

_____

_____

_____

_____

_____

_____

_____

_____

_____

_____

When You Are Stuck, Reframe

Alice and Bud had four children between them; they each brought two from their previous marriages. Bud's ex-wife refused to work, and Alice's ex-husband didn't make much money. Consequently, Alice and Bud both worked and each took care of his or her own respective children. Alice was exhausted, angry, and resentful much of the time. She couldn't force her ex-husband to work, and Bud was doing the best he could. Alice felt trapped and depressed with no end in sight. Although she knew it wasn't rational, at times she resented her stepkids because if they weren't there, Bud would have been able to help support her and her children. They could have had a simpler life. She felt guilty whenever she had these feelings. One night, Alice was venting behind closed doors and the teenagers in the house overheard her complaints. The kids called a family meeting. They thanked their parents for working so hard to support their family and asked how they could help. For Alice and Bud, it was like a miracle. The kids started doing more chores around the house, and two of them got part-time jobs.

Bud wasn't as surprised at this turn of events as Alice. He had believed in their blended family all along. But with renewed hope, Alice's perspective shifted. Instead of feeling trapped, she felt good about her contribution to her family.

It's Not Always What You Think

Little George was only five when his mother remarried. Roberta and Carlos were young and deeply in love. Roberta had been a single mother for five years and felt good about creating a two-parent family for George. He had always been a good boy—quiet and mild-mannered.

George stayed with his Aunt Mary while his parents went on their honeymoon. Roberta and Carlos discussed parenting on their trip and decided on new rules for the home. When they returned, they immediately implemented the new rules feeling certain that the more stable, two-parent family would be good for George.

As new lovers tend to be, Carlos and Roberta were absorbed with each other. One day, the school principal called Roberta to come get George. He had slugged another boy in his first-grade class. When Roberta asked George what had happened, he hung his head and said he didn't know. At dinner that night, Carlos tried to tell George that hitting was unacceptable and not to do it anymore. George stormed off into his room.

After that day, George didn't get into trouble again but withdrew into his shell more with each passing day. Since he had always been a quiet boy, Roberta and Carlos didn't really notice. They were so enthralled with each other that George became invisible. As long as he didn't get into trouble or make a fuss, they thought things were fine.

It wasn't until George was a young man that he found his words. He finally communicated to his mother how anxious and abandoned he had felt as a boy. His parents had been so preoccupied with their own happiness, they had assumed that things were fine for the entire family.

Even as a young adult, it was helpful for George to tell his parents how he felt and to receive their understanding and care. They apologized for being blind to his emotions at the time. Their relationships improved from that point on.

Tips for Tending to Your Relationships
- Take time to check in with each child and your spouse to see how things are going for them.
- Pay special attention to their emotional and behavioral reactions during the transition to a new household.
- Help your children talk about what they are experiencing.
- Talking about feelings doesn't need to result in external changes, but it helps create more connection and safety in the relationship.
- Taking time to notice and listen with an open heart builds trust.

Second-Class Citizens
Between the two of them, Rhea and Zack had five children when they married. Rhea felt very protective of her children during the transition. They had moved into Zack's house, and his daughters were admittedly territorial about their space. Right from the get-go, Rhea felt like a second-class citizen in the house and she assumed that her kids did, too. Zack wasn't around all that much because he was working to support the whole family. But when he was with the family he spread his attention and affection evenly among the kids.

Rhea felt overwhelmed with managing all of the kids' needs. Her default position was her biological children. Zack's kids complained to their dad about their stepmom, landing Zack smack-dab in the middle of his wife and his kids. Rhea felt so drained by the situation that it was hard to hear Zack's concerns. She heard them as criticisms and felt defensive and attacked. Rhea began withdrawing from her stepchildren and asking Zack to take more responsibility for their care. This was hard because Zack was the provider and didn't have the time or energy to tend to many of his kids' needs. Rhea made sack lunches for her kids to take to school but required her stepkids to buy their lunch at school. She took her own kids to dance classes and baseball practices and arranged carpools for her stepkids. Tensions between the stepsiblings rose, as they became competitors rather than part of the same family team.

The kids argued and teased each other. The parents felt obligated to take sides, and feelings of alienation grew all over the place. Family counseling ensued. It took some time to unwind all the different issues with so many people, but in the end individuals were able to open up with understanding and empathy for each other. Rhea realized that amidst her resentment about being a second-class citizen, she had inadvertently treated her stepchildren as just that.

Points to Ponder
- There is an innate protective instinct toward one's own biological children.
- Even so, try to be "biologically blind" with your love as best you can.
- Offer consideration and respect equally, whether they are bio-kids or stepkids.

EXERCISES

1. What are your beliefs about your relationships with your partner, stepkids, children, and others? Our beliefs help create our thoughts, especially the subconscious ones that we are not fully aware of having. Write down the first thing that comes to mind.

I believe that my partner

_____

_____

_____

I believe that my stepchildren

_____

_____

_____

I believe that my stepchildren will never

_____

_____

_____

2. Now take a look at what you've written above. Ask yourself the following questions:

Are your beliefs accurate?

Are they realistic?

Are they positive and encouraging so that you feel good when you think about them?

Or are they negative and make you feel down or distressed?

3. We have the option of changing our perspective and our beliefs. Try answering the same questions below in a positive way that you would like to be true. Make sure the statements are positive and uplifting. For example, "I believe that my stepchildren love me."

I believe that my partner:

_____

_____

_____

I believe that my stepchildren:

_____

_____

_____

I believe that my stepchildren will never:

_____

_____

_____

4. What corresponding actions can you take that would help turn these positive beliefs into reality?

_____

_____

_____

_____

_____

5. When our present experience is stressful to us, it is usually because it is shaking up our internal reality map in some way. All of us have our personal life stories, which color the way we see our current world. What is your story? Have you decided that your situation is unfair or disappointing or that people are generally untrustworthy or unkind? What are your beliefs about your family? What are your fears? Are they based on today's reality, or are they based on old experiences and hurts? Take a moment and think about this question. Don't think too hard, just write down the first answer that comes to mind.

What do I believe about people in my life in general?

_____

_____

_____

_____

_____

_____

_____

_____

6. How do your beliefs (in the last exercise) affect your relationship with your stepchildren and spouse?

_____

_____

_____

_____

_____

_____

_____

_____

_____

_____

Points to Ponder
- Notice if you are paying more attention to what you think you haven't done right than what you have done well.
- Once you are aware of this, try focusing on your positive traits and what you have done well. Try talking to yourself as you would to your very best friend.
- If your best friend was feeling poorly and struggling, you would try to boost him up. You would tell him about his positive qualities and his good deeds.

EXERCISES

1. List three positives about yourself with regard to your family. (If you can't think of any, write down three positive qualities that you would like to develop in yourself.)

_____

_____

_____

_____

_____

_____

2. Write down a present-tense statement of how you want things to be, for example: "We have a loving, peaceful blended family."

_____

_____

_____

_____

_____

_____

_____

3. Close your eyes and pretend the affirmation you wrote in #2 is true right now. For example, imagine what it feels like for the statement "We have a loving, peaceful blended family" to be true. Let's say it feels warm, safe, fun, and comforting. Practice that feeling while repeating to yourself, "We have a loving, peaceful blended family."

This is a powerful exercise that helps to expand your comfort zone. The more you focus on your affirmations, the more you will notice and create opportunities to make this your reality.

Try it. It usually works.

Chapter Ten

The ABCs of Resiliency

*"Most of the important things in the world have been accomplished by
people who have kept on trying when there seemed to be no hope at all."*
—DALE CARNEGIE

Before we can help our families deal with life's curveballs, we
must cultivate our own personal resiliency. It's like the safety
demonstration given at the start of every commercial airline flight—
the flight attendant demonstrates how to put on the oxygen mask
in case of a sudden drop in cabin pressure, stressing that parents
should put their own mask on before assisting their children.

"Accept things as they come, and make the most of it. Keep
your life on the up and up," advised a couple, who were happily
married and each 101 years old. As do most centenarians, they
credited their longevity to their attitude in life. Dr. Thomas Perls of
the Boston University School of Medicine has studied centenarians
for over eleven years. He says, "The preliminary data is that these
folks manage stress very well. It isn't so much the amount of stress
in their lives that matters; it's that they manage it well. They don't
dwell on things. They seem to be able to let go."

When I married my husband and became a stepmother, I was eager to develop close relationships with my stepdaughters. But things didn't go as quickly as I might have wanted; rather than jumping in with both feet to instant stepmotherhood, I had to slow down and allow us all to become comfortable with each other, and to grow a natural rapport over time. While each of us adjusted to our new circumstances, I felt more inspired than ever to be a stabilizing force in my new family. As someone who has always been easily knocked off balance, I needed to get better at going with the flow and focusing my energy on what I could control versus what I couldn't. My husband is an exceptionally resilient person. He regains his balance quickly and doesn't dwell on things that he can't change (a strong trait of resilient people). I needed to learn resiliency skills for my own well-being and to be able to keep moving forward. Resiliency comes naturally to some people, but the good news for the rest of us is that it's a skill that can be learned!

Tips for Resiliency

- Choose an optimistic outlook on life.
- Have a realistic and broad perspective.
- See beyond yourself—don't personalize.
- Manage stress well.
- Focus on what you have control over instead of what you don't.
- Let go of things you can't change.
- Don't dwell on the negative.
- Focus on and strengthen the positive.
- Accept others as they are, but have clear limits on what kind of treatment you will tolerate.
- Commit to taking care of your life and daily duties even when you don't feel like it.

Your Thinking Style Determines Your Resiliency

"It is thinking style that determines resilience—more than genetics, more than intelligence, more than any other single factor."
—KAREN REIVICH AND ANDREW SHATTE

Did you know that the average person has up to 10,000 thoughts every day? How tuned in are you to the thoughts running through your own mind? We all have a tipping point at which our energy gets overwhelmed by negative or positive thoughts; you can intentionally choose which direction you want to go if you pay close attention.

Randal hoped that his stepson Alex would come to work with him in his company when he graduated from college. Randal needed the help and hoped that one day Alex might even take over the company. Randal offered Alex—then a teenager—a part-time job so that he could start learning the business.

However, Alex declined the job offer. Randal took it personally, inferring that Alex didn't want the job because he didn't want to be that closely involved with his stepdad. Randal could have asked Alex why he didn't want the job, but instead, his feelings were hurt and he backed off from their relationship. The way we think and choose to interpret events has a lot to do with how resilient we are.

For example, Randal could have looked at Alex's decision a few different ways. He could have decided that Alex didn't want to work with him because he was lazy and ungrateful. He could have decided that Alex wasn't interested in that field. Alternatively, Randal could have concluded Alex just didn't want to spend so much time with his stepfather. The reality was that Alex was simply not interested in his stepdad's business and was enjoying his internship in computer science. Being an adolescent boy at the time, Alex didn't think to tell his stepfather why he wasn't interested. Because Randal assumed it was personal toward him, he withdrew from the relationship instead of just asking his stepson about it. Alex felt the tension with his stepfather and withdrew in turn because he felt awkward and didn't know what to make of it.

Resilient people generally display the following characteristics:
- They are less likely to alienate people.
- They have stable relationships.
- They tend to be healthier and happier.
- They go slowly and build new family connections over time.

Don't Jump to Conclusions

Ronnie was continually upset about the way her stepdaughter Ashley treated Ronnie's two children. Ashley was only a year older than her twin stepsisters, and she consistently ignored them. They were always asking her to play with them, but Ashley refused. The twins would cry to their mom and sulk because their stepsister didn't seem to like them. Ronnie racked her brains, trying to figure out why Ashley was so negative toward herself and her girls. And then it occurred to her: Ashley's mother had always blamed Ronnie as the cause of her divorce from her husband. The ex-wife must have persuaded Ashley to resist acceptance of her new family. Ronnie felt angry, and Ashley could feel a coolness come over their relationship

Within six months, Ashley began inventing excuses for not coming over. Joshua, her dad, missed her and started taking her out to dinner for some daddy-daughter time. Ashley didn't sleep over at their house anymore.

During his alone time with his daughter (coupled with some lengthy discussions with his ex-wife), Joshua discovered what was really going on. It turned out that the root of the problem was Ashley's shyness. She was excruciatingly shy (born that way— genetics play a big role in how introverted or extroverted we are). Shy people are often misunderstood and thought to be socially avoidant, aloof, uninterested, or uncaring, but just like everyone else in the family, Susan craved acceptance and love. She longed for safe connections and a sense of belonging.

With this new understanding, Ronnie and Ashley began a new chapter, which spilled over to the other children. Ronnie was especially gentle and encouraging toward Ashley and taught her children to do the same. They learned to develop their relationship at her pace without taking her shyness as reluctance to be with them. Understanding one another is a beautiful and helpful thing. Ashley slowly warmed up and became more comfortable. It turned out that she had a playful, creative streak and sparked a lot of fun times for the whole family!

EXERCISES

1. Write down a negative reaction that you had to some recent experience or event.

_____

_____

_____

_____

2. How did you interpret the event that you reacted to?

_____

_____

_____

_____

_____

3. What are your beliefs around the experience? Write them down for future reference.

_____

_____

_____

_____

_____

4. How sure are you that your interpretation is accurate? Circle one:

100%   75%   50%   25%   5%   0%

If it's possible to check with the relevant parties and test your level of accuracy, do so. It could be an interesting learning experience.

Resiliency skills can help you
- notice how your emotions and behavior stem from how you look at things;
- always check for accuracy in your thinking;
- discover another way to look at a situation that entirely changes its meaning; and
- change your perspective or understanding in ways that can improve your ability to cope with stress.

Neuroscientists have found that when young people learn to handle stress, this mastery becomes imprinted in their neural circuitry, leaving them more resilient when facing stress as adults. Many teenagers enjoy horror movies; after experiencing cinematic terror and emerging intact from the theater, they feel good about having endured and overcome the intense emotional experience. While most divorce is not quite "horrifying," it can be frightening and disorienting to kids. As stepparents, we are part of a life-changing experience for the children. If we are mindful about patiently assisting their adjustment, we can help them develop resiliency.

Resilient stepparents
- focus on what they can do something about, not what they can't change;
- are able to cope better with stress;
- bounce back faster;
- have more self-confidence, are more cooperative, and capable of forgiveness; and
- model resilience for the people around them.

EXERCISES

1. Think about something that you had a negative reaction to and write down how you saw it:

Adversity:

_____

_____

_____

_____

_____

Beliefs:

_____

_____

_____

_____

_____

Consequences:

_____

_____

_____

_____

_____

2. How certain are you of the accuracy of your beliefs as they pertain to this specific instance? Circle one:

Not Certain   Somewhat Certain   Absolutely Certain

3. What might be a more accurate interpretation than your first one?

_____

_____

_____

_____

_____

Adversity:

_____

_____

_____

_____

_____

Beliefs:

_____

_____

_____

_____

_____

Consequences:

_____

_____

_____

_____

_____

Chapter Eleven

Happiness: A Scientific Approach

*You cannot capture happiness no matter how much you
chase after it. Happiness is something that follows you;
it follows your positive actions."*
—DAISAKU TKEDA

Elena had struggled with depression for most of her life. When
she became a mother, she found her bliss. Raising her children
was the happiest time in her life. But when the kids grew up and
went away to college, she had a rude awakening. First she found out
her husband of twenty-two years was unhappy and wanted a divorce.
And then her depression came back with a vengeance. Nothing in
Elena's life could fill the void created by the absence of her children.
She limped along for a couple of years until she met Richard.

Richard had dated women who ultimately broke up with him
because they didn't want to deal with someone else's children. To
his surprise, Elena was eager to step into the role of being a second
mother to his children. He was delighted to find someone who
embraced motherhood the way Elena did.

They had a short courtship and a small wedding. Richard and Elena adapted quickly to family life together. Elena happily started cooking for the kids and taking them to their sporting events. She enjoyed watching her nine-year-old stepson, Roger, play in his soccer matches and her eleven-year-old stepdaughter Madison dance at her recitals.

Roger ignored Elena's presence at the games despite her jumping and cheering when he scored a goal. And one day, Madison politely asked Elena not to stay and watch her dance because it was embarrassing. "It's awkward enough that my mom comes to watch me dance sometimes. I don't mean to hurt your feelings, but I really don't need another adult embarrassing me!"

Elena hung in there, working at the relationships for several years, until the depression returned. She was deeply sad and disappointed that her new family wasn't working out the way she had expected. Her husband Richard gently tried to get Elena to see that the kids were teenagers and they wanted as little as possible to do with the adults in their lives. It was a phase: two parents were more than enough for them.

Elena tried to accept things as they were and focused on building a life with Richard. Eventually, Elena got a job in a preschool working with children. Her job brought her more pleasure and meaning than she had felt in years. Richard and Elena learned to play bridge and developed a whole social network around it. Elena found that even though she was prone to depression, she could significantly influence her happiness by choosing activities that brought her pleasure, full engagement, and meaning.

We Have More Control Over Our Happiness Than We Think[6]

- Approximately 50 percent of our happiness level is genetically determined.
- Life circumstances determine about 10 percent.

---

6 Portions of this list and the next were excerpted and paraphrased from *The How of Happiness: A Scientific Approach to Getting the Life You Want*, by Sonja Lyubomirsky, PhD.

- Intentional activities determine 40 percent.
- As a stepparent, not only can you take charge of your own happiness, but also your happiness, or lack of it, will spill over to the rest of your family.

Thinking and Behavior Patterns Found in the Happiest People

- They devote a great amount of time to their family and friends, nurturing and enjoying these relationships.
- They are comfortable expressing gratitude for all they have.
- They are often the first to offer a helping hand to coworkers and passersby.
- They practice optimism when imagining their futures.
- They savor life's pleasures and try to live in the present moment.
- They make physical exercise a weekly and even daily habit.
- They are deeply committed to lifelong goals and ambitions.
- They demonstrate poise and strength when coping with challenges.

Cultivate Your Own Happiness

When John married Anna, he wanted a family. He had reached the age of fifty-two without marrying or fathering any children. He was excited to have her two daughters in his life. Their biological father lived on the other side of the country. He didn't pay child support or have regular contact with the kids. When the father did talk to his daughters, it usually included moaning to them about their mother and how she had the law pursuing him for money when he didn't have any. He would plead with them to intervene and try to get their mother to stop asking him for child support. Needless to say, these conversations were painful for his daughters; it wasn't until years later that they became strong enough to stand up to their biological father. Eventually, the oldest daughter stopped talking to her dad, and the younger one insisted that he stop putting her in the middle.

When John came on the scene, he swooped into the father void. He happily did things with his stepdaughters and took them places. He bought them things and tried to be the attentive father that they didn't have. His ten-year-old stepdaughter Cara accepted his gestures and bonded with him, but the fourteen-year-old, Neta, was less welcoming. She didn't want anything to do with her father or her stepfather. John persevered, thinking the older girl would eventually come around. Meanwhile, his relationship with Anna blossomed as they settled into their marriage. After three years, John's stepdaughters accepted him but continued to keep their distance in their own ways. John would try to be friendly toward the now seventeen-year-old.

"How was your date?" he'd ask her the next morning after she'd been out with her boyfriend.

"Kids don't date. And please don't ask me such stupid questions first thing in the morning. It puts me in a bad mood for the rest of the day."

No matter how many times his oldest stepdaughter spoke to him like this, John was still shocked into silence. It helped that she spoke to her mom the same way at times, but she didn't do it as often and she also had a loving relationship with her mom at other times.

Even though his younger stepdaughter Cara was more receptive to spending time with John, she remained fiercely loyal to her father. She would defend her father and run to her room crying if anyone said anything negative about him. Even though John understood at some level that Cara was hurting and doing her best to cope with the situation, it aggravated him that the father had unconditional devotion from Cara while John continued to have limited access to her heart. Alas, this is often the blight of being a stepparent. It goes with the territory. It's an ongoing balance to keep one's heart open and engaged and not take the pullbacks or pushbacks too personally. While he felt like an outsider at times, he enjoyed spending time with the girls and being a family; it brought him joy, even if his feelings weren't always reciprocated.

Cultivating Happiness

"People are only as happy as they make up their minds to be."
—ABRAHAM LINCOLN

When their world is a safe and predictable place, children feel more secure and confident. It can help your stepchildren to feel loved, safe, and accepted if you take the time to get to know them. What are their interests and thoughts about the world around them? Look for ways that your interests dovetail so that you can do things together that you both enjoy.

Nikki came to see me for psychotherapy because she was depressed about her family situation. She was married, with one biological child and two stepchildren. The mother was not very involved; she lived in another city, and the children visited her a few times a year. Nikki was frustrated because her stepkids didn't listen to her. She also felt her husband, Vance, undermined her efforts to discipline them. Vance's view was that she was too harsh with the kids (especially his). He was raised in an abusive home and was very sensitive to his children being reprimanded.

Nikki was at her wits' end. The more frustrated and angry she got, the shorter her fuse became. Her husband became less and less supportive of her authority. The children exploited this rift between the adults by complaining to Dad about Nikki when he got home at the end of the day. In first families, if a child complains about one parent to the other, the adults take it in stride. But in a blended family, when biological children cry mistreatment by their stepparent, relationships can suffer. While it's natural for parents to have a wired-in protective instinct regarding their children, couples need honest communication and teamwork to manage conflicts successfully. Nikki had the responsibility of caring for the children full-time without the necessary authority, which she found incredibly stressful. Finally, Vance and Nikki decided to pursue couples counseling.

First, they had to listen to each other and understand their experiences together. Then they worked to mend their fences and become a unified team. They negotiated the ground rules of the household and found areas where they could agree. They decided Nikki would ask the children to behave, and if they didn't listen, Vance would step in as reinforcement. This way, Nikki wouldn't get overly frustrated and irritable, and end up pushing her husband's buttons. Nikki felt supported, and the children got the structure they sorely needed.

Even though Nikki was now getting additional support from Vance, she still found herself becoming irritable and resentful. She felt like the children idolized their absent mother, while Nikki did the grunt work. The mother was the recipient of the children's affections, while Nikki was the target of their anger. Since her feelings for her own son were less complicated, she doted on him. Her stepchildren felt the difference in how their stepmom favored their half brother and acted out to get attention from Nikki.

After some soul-searching, Nikki decided to turn things around. She began focusing on the positive aspects of her family. She appreciated the opportunity to be a stay-at-home mom, something she had always wanted. She was grateful for her husband, a loyal, loving family man. Over time, Nikki made a conscious decision to fully open her heart to her stepkids. They felt her change of heart and responded by softening toward her. When Nikki embraced her stepkids (with a lot of support from her husband), their relationships all blossomed and inspired more individual and collective happiness.

The happiest people
- want what they have;
- are more kind and generous with other people; and
- tend to be healthier, more successful, and have better relationships.

We can always find something positive and desirable in our situation. For example, sometimes I wish my husband and I had more time to spend with his daughters. There is only so much that either he or I can do about this—besides, the girls are at an age

110

where it is healthy for them to be more interested in their friends than being with their family. The silver lining in our situation is we have more alone time to enjoy each other's company. Because our time with the girls is limited, we are inspired to try and make the most of every minute of family time.

The Link Between Kindness and Happiness

Engaging in acts of kindness can actually increase your happiness level. In order to for this to work, you have to vary your acts of kindness. For example, if you regularly visit the elderly lady down the street, or go out of your way to cater to the eating preferences of the kids, these kind behaviors don't qualify as a happiness/kindness exercise. At least once a week, carry out a kind act that is outside your normal routine. For instance, you could send a care package to your stepdaughter who has the flu at college, or volunteer to help your partner's ex with a chore.

EXERCISES

1. For two weeks, keep a journal of what you did that day and rate your day in terms of your happiness and satisfaction on a scale of 1–10. After two weeks, go back and look at your scores and notice which activities consistently accompany your more positive days. This is a great tool for taking responsibility for your own happiness.

Research shows that people who participate each day in activities that bring them pleasure, a sense of engagement (lose-track-of-time kind of thing), and meaning are happier. Do the following exercises to help you determine what activities you can intentionally do to increase your happiness level.

2. Write down five pleasurable activities that you can do with your stepchildren and/or your spouse (e.g., making chocolate chip cookies, going to a ball game, going for a walk).

_____

_____

_____

_____

_____

_____

_____

3. Ask your children and stepchildren for ideas about things they would enjoy doing together as a family. Such activities can help you get to know them better and support them with their interests.

4. Which activities bring you a sense of personal fulfillment (and cause you to lose track of time when you are doing them)? This kind of experience is called "being in the flow," and can be the same as the activities that give you pleasure:

_____

_____

_____

_____

_____

_____

_____

5. Which activities in your life give you a sense of meaning? That is, they are personally fulfilling or contribute to the lives around you.

_____

_____

_____

_____

_____

_____

_____

6. Now, try these exercises with your spouse and then your children and/or stepchildren. It will help you get to know each other better. You can encourage your spouse and children to build their "happiness activities" into their daily life. Try to participate in activities that bring you pleasure, fulfillment, and meaning every day. These are different for each person, but research shows that when you do this, you are likely to be happier.

Chapter Twelve

Optimism and Gratitude

"Optimism is not about providing a recipe for self-deception. The world can be a horrible, cruel place, and at the same time it can be wonderful and abundant. These are both truths. There is not a halfway point; there is only choosing which truth to put in your personal foreground."
—LEE ROSS

When Jack married Theresa, his friends and family warned him about the difficultly of becoming a stepfather to teenage kids. Everyone cautioned him to have low expectations. His own children lived with him 20 percent of the time, and his stepchildren were there 80 percent of the time. From the beginning, he worried his own boys would resent that he spent more time with his stepsons than he did with his own children. In an effort to protect his sons from being hurt, he kept a distance from his stepchildren. He convinced himself that they already had their own dad and didn't really need him.

Jack missed his own children terribly, and his stepsons reminded him of their absence. He felt guilty about the divorce and sad to see so little of his sons. Theresa tried to explain her husband's moodiness to her sons, and luckily for Jack, they were good-natured, optimistic kids. They had a good relationship with their own father and they seemed to understand Jack's sadness and cut him some slack. But Jack felt like his family was broken, and he didn't believe Humpty Dumpty could be put back together again. He didn't have the heart to try very hard with his own sons or stepsons. He had always been a bit of a pessimist, anticipating the worst possible outcome and then planning accordingly. For example, he loved to play golf. But he hardly ever played because he didn't think that he'd ever be a very good golfer. He avoided the game because he anticipated always being disappointed in how he played.

Without dismissing the challenges of blended families, you may find that sometimes they can work a lot better than you might anticipate. I encourage you to try and see what is really happening in your relationships—for better or worse—without clouding the view with your fears and self-protective blanket.

Not long after Jack and Theresa got married, Jack's fifteen-year-old stepson Allan won two tickets to a baseball game. He invited his father. When his dad canceled and Allan invited Jack, Jack felt lukewarm about the invitation; he saw himself as the second or last choice and believed he always would be. If Jack were a realist, he would have viewed the invitation as an opportunity to do something fun with his stepson. And if he were an optimist, he would have seen it as the first of many opportunities to bond with his stepson. He would have looked at the baseball game as a starting point for building a meaningful relationship. Instead, as a pessimist anticipating the worst possible outcome, he declined the invitation because, without fully realizing it, he was protecting himself from getting close to his stepson. He didn't believe that stepfamilies could blend in a positive way. To his surprise, Allan invited his stepbrother, Jack's oldest son. The two of them went and had a jolly time together.

During the first year of Jack and Theresa's marriage, the boys all formed friendships, each one unique in its own right. Jack's boys were fourteen and twelve, and his stepsons were fifteen and twelve. The two older boys both enjoyed shooting hoops and skateboarding together.

The two younger boys were both in Little League—they practiced pitching and hitting together in their front yard. In the evening, they played the video game *Backyard Baseball* together. Jack's fourteen-year-old taught his twelve-year-old stepbrother to skateboard, and his own twelve-year-old looked up to his gifted fifteen-year-old stepbrother, who shared his interest in science. They ran experiments together with their chemistry set—causing an explosion one time that had the whole household running to see what had happened.

As the boys all grew closer, Jack's sons had sleepovers with their stepbrothers and they all wanted to go on family vacations together. Jack actually ended up seeing his own sons more often because of his stepsons. Their new family began to take a shape of its own—with the remarriage eventually adding much more to the kids' lives than the divorce had taken away.

Optimism as an Orientation-in-Thinking Plus

Optimism is not merely positive thinking, with pessimism being just negative thinking, they are orientations in thinking—ways that we explain things to ourselves. So, if things are not going well for Jack, as a pessimist, he assumes his life will continue that way. When something positive happens to Jack, he credits it to luck and assumes it's a temporary situation. In contrast, when things go well for an optimist, he or she generalizes it and expects it to continue into the future. Optimists think of negative events as temporary and specific to a particular moment. Pessimism can create a feeling of helplessness—a sense that no matter what you do, nothing will change for the better. Therefore, pessimistic people may more easily stop trying or not even try in the first place.

Characteristics of Optimistic People
- Optimistic people have better relationships.
- Optimistic people have more successful marriages.
- Optimistic people are more productive and tend to live an average of nine years longer than people with pessimistic outlooks.

On Gratitude

Madeline was lying in bed on a holiday weekend, stewing about the fact that her husband's ex-wife had been calling them constantly. She and her husband had been working on this issue for as long as they had been married. Merck didn't want to confront his ex-wife, because he didn't want to ruffle her feathers or hurt her feelings. Meanwhile, Madeline was stewing. So, Madeline lay in bed, thinking about all the times over the past three years that the ex-wife had intruded into their lives and Merck had not stopped her. Madeline was angry and resentful; she found herself thinking she might want to spend the day alone or with a friend instead of being with her husband as they had planned. She became aware of her chest hurting, an angina-like pain in her heart. She felt even angrier thinking about how this situation was wearing on her spirit and her health. She felt tired and grouchy. After thirty minutes of lying in bed, listing all of her grievances in her mind, she pulled the covers over her head and lay there feeling terrible, with a continuous sharp pain in her heart.

Merck felt caught between his ex-wife and his new wife. Madeline complained that Merck accommodated his ex-wife at their inconvenience and then didn't stand up for his new wife. Merck tried to explain that he was doing it for his children. He didn't want them caught in the middle of bickering parents. They'd had their fill of that when their parents had been married. Merck's ex-wife had a difficult, high-conflict personality. He'd learned to pick and choose his battles carefully and minimize engagement whenever possible.

Madeline had been working hard on self-awareness and harnessing the power of her mind to affect her attitude and physical health. In her therapy, Madeline had been trying to learn new breathing and thinking habits to take the place of her tendency to focus on the negative. As she lay in bed trying to take deep, slow breaths and quiet her mind, her thoughts swerved to a special aunt of hers. She had always admired her aunt for her consistent ability to bounce back from difficult times. Madeline wondered if she would appear foolish to her aunt if she asked for some advice on this matter; maybe her feelings about the ex-wife were unreasonable. Maybe she was making too much out of it and causing her own suffering. Her sage aunt would give her honest opinion. Was Madeline being a doormat, letting everyone walk all over her? Or was she being too thin-skinned about the calls? Madeline knew in her heart the ex-wife was not a threat to her and that her husband was devoted to his new wife in every way. What would auntie say? The sharp angina pain in her heart got stronger, and Madeline thought she could die from the stress. She thought something serious must be happening to her heart to cause that much pain. She felt sorry for herself. Then her thoughts went to her mother; how would she feel if her daughter died before she did?

Madeline then realized how lucky her family had been, because there had not been any deaths other than grandparents. Her family had not suffered the death of any members "out of chronological order." She knew that experience could be devastating for families. Madeline started thinking about how fortunate both her family of origin and her blended family had been—no major tragedies. Too many families, she thought, have to cope with terminally ill children or tragic accidents in which young people are lost. Energy akin to gratitude and love began filling her chest cavity. She found herself taking deep breaths and celebrating the good fortune in her family; they were really lucky. Then she noticed how differently she felt. Her body was light, buoyant; the pain her chest was gone, and she felt energized and positive. She decided that she was giving the situation with the ex-wife too much power and that she had the ability to choose where she put her mental focus.

Madeline began to make a habit of refocusing her attention on the things she felt grateful for—this improved both her physical and mental well-being. She started with her biggest area of resentment, which was Merck's ex-wife.

Madeline started a list of things she felt grateful for:

- gratitude to her husband's ex-wife for not interfering in her relationship with her stepsons;
- gratitude to her husband's ex-wife for divorcing her husband so that Madeline could be with him;
- gratitude to her husband's ex-wife for the rare times that she did seem to be trying to be cooperative and friendly; and
- gratitude to her husband's ex-wife for being a challenging personality for her husband to deal with, making Madeline look easy in comparison.

Madeline's renewed focus on the positive didn't always make the negative feelings or frustrations go away. But it did make it easier for her to deal with difficult situations when they occurred. When Madeline talked with her husband, her upset was tempered by the gratitude work that she had been doing. She was able to talk about her dissatisfaction over the number of calls from his ex-wife in a calm and rational way. Instead of feeling overwhelmed by her anger and frustration, Merck could actually take in her complaints. Most often, he saw the middle ground and was able to reassure Madeline that they would work together to establish better boundaries with his ex-wife.

Dr. Laura King, a professor at the University of Missouri-Columbia, came up with the "Best Possible Self" exercise. In her study, King directed participants to write for twenty minutes per day, for four days in a row, about their best possible future selves. A control group wrote about other topics. She found that people who wrote about their positive self-vision for twenty minutes for several days, as compared to the control group, experienced higher levels of happiness several weeks later, as well as decreases in physical ailments that had been reported at the beginning of the study.

Here's how the "Best Possible Self" exercise works: imagine what your best possible future self will be like in several different areas of your life. Picture your life as if all your dreams had come true, and your highest potential realized.

EXERCISES

1. Your Best Possible Self Exercise: Take twenty minutes and write in a notebook about your best possible relationship with your spouse, children, stepchildren, and extended family. You can jot some notes down here.

_____
_____
_____
_____
_____
_____
_____
_____
_____

Then on a different day if you like, write down the steps and small goals needed to get you there.

_____
_____
_____
_____
_____
_____
_____
_____
_____

This exercise can help you hone your optimism skills. When you find yourself having negative thoughts about your ability to create your best possible self, recognize these thoughts for what they are. It may be that your vision of your best possible self is not realistic, and in that case, you can redesign it in a way that could work. It can be helpful to write down your negative thoughts and then replace them with more realistic and optimistic ones.

2. Three Positive Reflections Exercise:[7] Every night before you go to sleep, think of three positive things that happened during the day. They can be big or small, just things that you feel grateful about or are glad happened. This exercise can help you feel happier, less depressed, and more optimistic. It can also build skills of remembering and focusing on good events, gratitude, and life satisfaction.

3. Write down three positive things about your stepkids.

_____

_____

_____

_____

_____

4. Write down three positive things about your spouse.

_____

_____

_____

_____

_____

7 Christopher Peterson and Martin E. P. Seligman, *Character Strengths and Virtues: A Handbook and Classification* (New York: Oxford University Press and Washington, DC: American Psychological Association, 2004).

Chapter Thirteen

Building Lasting Relationships

"In the cherry blossom's shade, there is no such thing as a stranger."
—JAPANESE POET ISSA, 1763–1828

*"The goal of life is a deep state of well-being and wisdom at all moments,
accompanied by love for every being. True happiness arises from the
essential goodness that whole-heartedly desires everyone to find meaning in
their lives. It is a love that is always available, without showiness or
self-interest—the immutable simplicity of a good heart."*
—MATTHIEU RICARD

Helping Relationships Blossom

Angie and Donald had been married for one year, and Angie
longed to get pregnant. Donald had two boys from a previous
marriage (ages six and ten) and Angie didn't have any children
of her own. She was frustrated about having to wait to begin
her new family with Donald until the legal battle with David's
ex-wife settled down. Angie was a special education teacher for
kindergarten-age children and was quite gifted at her work.

Donald's ex-wife was suing to gain more custody of the boys. They had a fifty-fifty arrangement, but the mom claimed her boys were not safe if left alone with their stepmother. She insisted they could not be left with Angie for more than four hours at a time. Angie was deeply offended because she was especially proud of her skills with children.

Angie noticed that whenever the boys came over to the house, she felt negatively toward them. She was happier when she was alone with her husband, their father. She became acutely aware of how bad it had gotten when a long-term girlfriend of hers was visiting for a weekend. Her friend commented to her about how her mood shifted darkly upon the arrival of the boys. In thinking about it, Angie realized she had even taken to closing the door of the boys' bedroom when they were not there. She wanted to block out their very existence because it was painful to her.

Angie's friend also observed that the boys seemed like they were trying to be friendly toward Angie. They even asked Angie and her friend if they wanted to play a game with them. Angie had been so focused on the negatives in the situation that she wasn't really seeing the boys clearly. She was letting her feelings toward their mother taint her relationship with the boys. Remember, what we focus on expands. Angie preoccupied herself with the negative, it loomed in the forefront of her mind, tainting her experiences. When Angie focused on creating positive moments with her stepsons, her good feelings grew. She began to see them as innocent bystanders who wanted everyone to get along. She observed the love they had for their dad, as well as the acceptance and warmth that they had toward her. She allowed herself to begin connecting with them and developing a sense of belonging as a family. She began attending their sporting events and cheering them on. While their relationships continued to be strained for some time, they were able to share some good and bonding experiences that helped pave the way to a more integrated family feeling.

Points to Ponder
- Relationships blossom when we celebrate each other's accomplishments and joys.
- Accurately expressing understanding for what another person is experiencing can help build closeness.
- Matching a person's enthusiasm for what he or she is sharing with us can help create a bonding experience.

One day, Angie's stepson Will ran into the house after school and told Angie excitedly that he had been selected to be the new pitcher! He was stoked!

Angie stopped what she was doing and said, "That's fantastic! I know how much you wanted to pitch! When do you start? Your dad's going to be so excited!" Angie mirrored Will's enthusiasm and let him know that she was right there with him and that what he cared about mattered to her. Later in the day, she brought it up again, suggesting that they all go out for an ice cream after dinner to celebrate. Bringing up the exciting news again later that day or the next day can help extend the positive feelings and help to make the most out of something good that happened in Will's life.

Being There for the Rough Spots

One day, Will came home from tryouts with a long face. He seemed upset.

"What's wrong, Will?" asked Angie.

Will didn't say anything—he just hung his head and picked at his fingernails. Angie stopped what she was doing and went over to him.

"What happened, Will?" she asked in a soft, slow voice. When someone you love is stressed out, it can help him or her calm down and feel safe if you speak in a slow, soft voice—as if you were rocking a baby or petting a timid kitty cat. It is reassuring—it helps the person feel that you are there for them.

Will peeked at Angie and said glumly, "Coach decided that my friend Mark should pitch for a while. He seems to have a better record than me."

"I'm so sorry, Will. I know how much you enjoyed pitching. You must be so disappointed," Angie replied.

Offering empathy can help the other person to handle his own emotions. Our brain actually changes in the midst of the experience of receiving empathy. Stepparents can have a huge effect on their stepchildren and spouses when they offer a safe and caring environment. It may not always be apparent, but know that you are helping create a supportive atmosphere for them.

More Points to Ponder
- It's a tricky balance to keep an open heart with low expectations woven in.
- We are social beings wired to connect.
- When children feel genuinely safe and cared about by their caregivers, it promotes a secure attachment.
- When children feel like they can count on their parental units to be there for them, they tend to be more resilient.
- Our relationships affect the way our brain works—and when we feel connected and safe in our relationships, we are more capable of learning, loving, and growing into healthy, effective adults.

Working with What You Have
When Ruth and Jim married, she had two children from a previous marriage and he had three. Jim and his stepkids got along from the start. Jim and Paul, their dad, also liked each other and struck up a friendship. Sometimes, the chemistry is just right, and within a couple of years, Jim and the kids were tight. Ruth's experience with her stepchildren was more complicated (as it often is for stepmothers). Jim's ex-wife, Kim, did not remarry, and she resented Ruth. Kim made life as difficult as she could for Ruth; she influenced the kids against Ruth and tried to undermine the new family's happiness.

Kim was still hurt and angry about her divorce with Jim even though Ruth had nothing to do with it. Sometimes when people are unhappy, it is a hard to accept the happiness of others. Kim did things like dropping the children off at the last moment before Jim and Ruth were supposed to leave for a romantic trip—saying that an emergency had come up. Another time, she came up with an excuse for why the kids couldn't go with Jim and Ruth on a family vacation—at the last minute. She put the kids in the middle, which of course was uncomfortable for them. They felt badly for their mom because she was alone.

Ruth did her best to work with the situation and hoped that someday Kim would get better. In this case, unfortunately, Kim never came around (at least, after twenty-five years, she had made no progress). But the children did. Over the years, Ruth and Jim developed an even closer bond amidst the challenges, and the children eventually grew up and saw how their mother's resentment hindered their relationship with their stepmother. As they went on to create their own families, Ruth had a hard time accepting their spouses because she had to share her kids with them. Naturally, this took a toll on their relationships and created some distance that had not been there before. The kids came to appreciate and understand their stepmother better for having hung in there all those years, never uttering a negative word about their mom.

When one of your stepchildren wins a big part in the school play, or your spouse lands an important account, be sure to stop and celebrate the moment. For example, "I'm so happy for you, Sam. I know how hard you have been working on this." Or "Congratulations, sweetie, I know how much you wanted that part in the play! I can't wait to come and see it!" It doesn't take a lot of time or energy to match your own enthusiasm to theirs, but it can go a long way toward cultivating a good relationship. In today's busy world, it's easy to be distracted by your own thoughts and to-do lists, and miss the opportunity to celebrate someone else's special moment. When you can, try to build on positive emotion in our families by paying close attention to any member who is sharing something he or she feels really good about. When you celebrate another person's positive experiences, it can help to create a close and warm bond with everyone who cares about that person.

Caring Through Actions

Jared's father was unreliable. He would tell Jared he was coming to see him and then fail to show up. Molly had watched her son have his heart broken repeatedly by his father since he was too little to remember. One of the things that she loved about her new partner Curt was his dependability. When he said he was going to do something, you could count on it.

Molly and Curt would watch six-year-old Jared waiting for his father to arrive—ever hopeful that his father would come as he had promised. Curt was very sensitive to the ongoing disappointments that Jared experienced regarding his father. He made a special point of always following through on any promises that he made to Jared. When Curt told Jared that he would be at his Little League game, Jared looked surprised and delighted to see him actually show up. Curt never said a negative word about Jared's father. Instead, he demonstrated his caring through his consistent actions.

Tips for Building Flourishing Relationships
- Make time to spend together.
- Express positive feelings.
- Show interest and enthusiasm when the other person has good news.
- Allow room for differences.
- Share hopes and dreams with each other.
- Be supportive and loyal.
- Hug (unless the child prefers to not be hugged, of course).

1. Think of a mutually enjoyable activity to do with each family member. And then do it.

2. Next time someone tells you something he or she is excited about, try to match that person's enthusiasm in your response with your facial expression, words, and energy.

3. When someone in your blended family behaves in a way that bothers you, try to think about what is underlying the behavior. What do you think is motivating this person? Try to have empathy for the person's perspective.

4. Try to stop and pay close attention when someone in your family wants to tell you something. Keep your mind from thinking about other things and stay focused on the family member 100 percent. To demonstrate your interest, ask the person two questions about whatever is on the person's mind.

Chapter Fourteen

Words Matter—Effective Communication

*"Out beyond ideas of wrong doing and right doing, there is a field.
I will meet you there."*
—RUMI

True Listening Is an Act of Love

Emily tells her mom, "I don't want you to share the intimate stuff that I tell you with Harvey. It's embarrassing to me." Harvey is Emily's stepfather.

Emily's mom empathizes with her daughter and says, "I understand you don't want me to share with Harvey the private things you tell me. I can see how it might embarrass you. I don't want you to feel uncomfortable."

True listening is an act of love; in doing so, we give the message that we honor and value the other person. Our children and spouse will be more receptive to our thoughts after we listen to theirs with an open heart and mind.

When communicating our thoughts to others, particularly when they involve a request, it's a good idea to take responsibility for our feelings.

James didn't like it when his wife Suzanne and her ex-husband changed the plans with the kids and then sprang it on him at the last minute. Suzanne responded better when James said, "I feel surprised and like an outsider in my own home when I show up after work to find that our plans with your kids have changed, and that instead of two nights from now, they will be with us tonight. I don't like coming home and not knowing ahead of time that your kids will be at our house," as opposed to "It's not very considerate that you change the plans without consulting me. How would you feel if I did that to you with my kids?"

Stop Smothering Me

Following is a letter from and response to a teenager who wrote into my advice column:

Dear Dr. Diana,

My stepdad is treating me like one of his children. I really like him and I don't want to hurt his feelings. How can I tell him to stop?
—Smothered Stepdaughter

Dear Smothered Stepdaughter,
How do we tell anyone whom we care about something he or she may not like? Try the "sandwich technique." First, say something positive (a slice of bread), then the difficult or negative thing (the peanut

Nonviolent Communication

Psychologist, Marshall Rosenberg created Nonviolent Communication, sometimes also called Compassionate Communication. NVC is a process that helps people discuss conflicts or differences in a way that promotes a peaceful exchange.

"Nonviolent Communication is an awareness discipline masquerading as a communication process."
—KIT MILLER

Below is the suggested approach for requesting something from one another when using NVC:

1. Describe your observation.
2. Identify your feeling.
3. Explain the reason for your feeling in terms of your needs.
4. State your request.

butter or meat or whatever) and then close with a positive (the other slice of bread). In your case, start by telling your stepdad the positive stuff that you like about him and that you appreciate how he cares about you. Then tell him what makes you uncomfortable. Start with the general idea, perhaps something like this: "I don't want you to treat me like I'm one of your kids." Then try to be as specific as possible. For example, you might say, "When you tell me that you love me, I feel uncomfortable and that I have to say it back," or maybe "I don't like it when you discipline me. I would really prefer that my mom do it." You could also describe the relationship you would like to have with your stepdad. For example, "I'd like us to be friends," or "I'd just like us to not be mean to each other." End the conversation on a positive note: "Thank you for talking with me," or "Thank you for being the kind of person I can talk to."

The adult chose to be a stepparent. Your stepfather chose to be in this situation, but you, the child, did not.

Example:

1. When you describe your observation, do so without criticizing or judging. For example: "We don't usually talk at all during the day when we are at work."

2. Identify your feeling and take responsibility for it rather than blaming any external circumstance for it: "I miss you when I don't talk to you all day," or "I feel sad when I don't talk to you all day."

3. Explain the reason for your feeling in terms of your needs: "I like feeling close and connected to each other. When we don't talk all day, I feel distant and disconnected."

4. State your request: "I would like to talk to you during the day even for a couple of minutes once or twice. I want to feel more connected and share our day with each other even when we are apart."

When using judgmental language, we tend to demand rather than request, and we expect other people to prove their love for us by doing what we want. With a heart-centered approach, we request rather than demand; we

Most stepparents are eager and ready to have a relationship with their stepkids, while it takes kids much longer to bond. It is important for a stepparent to be sensitive to a child's readiness and level of interest in having a relationship with him or her. It can also be challenging for stepparents to hold back love they feel for a child. An ongoing open dialogue can help develop a lifelong, healthy relationship.

You are lucky to have a stepparent who cares about you. Your stepdad is also lucky to have a caring stepchild who wants to avoid hurting his feelings. Even when blended family members don't like each other, basic courtesy and respect toward one another is important, all the way around. And it sounds like you already know that.

express our feelings and wants without criticizing, judging, or attacking.

Another example:

1. Observation: "Your ex-husband seems to be calling you to talk about things after 10 p.m. quite often lately."
2. Feeling: "I feel angry when he calls after 10 p.m."
3. Need: "I feel like our intimate time is being intruded on when that happens. I really need some private time with you daily where he isn't so much in our world."
4. Request for Action: "I'd feel much better if you could either ask him not to call after 9:30 p.m., or just not answer the phone after 9:30 p.m."

Another example:

A husband gets home and is frustrated that his stepkids left their dirty dishes stacked in the sink.

1. Observation: "When I come home after work, there are dirty dishes piled in the sink, and the counters are sticky."
2. Feeling: "I feel frustrated, irritated and exhausted when I come home and see the mess."
3. Need: "I need everyone to respect the fact that I work all day and need to come home to a clean house."
4. Request for Action: "I would like it if the dishes and counters are clean by the time I get home."

Responding to a refusal to your request involves empathy in four steps:

1. Describe the situation.
2. Guess the other person's feelings.
3. Guess the reason for that feeling, together with the unmet need; then let the person verify whether you have correctly understood.
4. Clarify the unmet need.

Here's another approach that offers acceptance and understanding without making a direct request:

1. "Your son hardly ever cleans up after himself when he is at our house. When we remind him or ask him to clean up his stuff, he doesn't listen or do it. And you are unwilling to give him any kind of consequences."
2. "You don't want your son to feel badly or be upset."
3. "You don't see him very often so when he is here with us, you want him to be happy. Therefore, you don't discipline him during his brief visits, is that right?"
4. "So, you want and need your son to feel good when he is with us and enjoy his time at our house. You want him to enjoy coming over and being with you."

There are no demands, criticisms, or requests at the end of the discussion. While this type of communication doesn't guarantee that you'll agree on things, it does set the stage for negotiation, compromise, and mutual respect.

Points to Ponder

- Try to be aware of your own biases, judgments, and opinions without being overly concerned about who is right and who is wrong.
- Rarely are things as clear-cut as we think.
- Let your love be stronger than your need to be right.

These techniques are good to have in your back pocket when you run into challenges with your kids or your spouse, or in other relationships. While not all problems can be resolved solely through effective communication, none can be solved without it.

A newly married stepmother, Sarah felt overwhelmed by the magnitude of the unresolved emotional and financial issues between her husband and his ex-wife, and wondered if her marriage would be able to survive. Multiple calls each day from Robert's ex-wife, Ann, were disrupting their life. Sarah pleaded with Robert to put limits on his ex-wife. But she heard a familiar tune: Robert felt guilty for demanding a divorce. He didn't want to alienate or hurt Ann any more than he already had. He sought to avoid conflict with his ex-wife as much as possible; but this was causing conflict between Sarah and Robert, which was frustrating for both of them.

Robert began keeping his conversations and emails with Ann as private as possible to avoid friction with Sarah. One night, Robert was on his computer emailing while Sarah awaited him in bed. When Robert came up, Sarah asked him if he had been emailing Ann. He denied it and appeared irritated. As Sarah's resentment built and Robert felt pressured and trapped between the two women, the new couple's romantic life waned.

Sarah learned to say "I feel," "I want," and "I need," rather than "you this or that," to Robert, which made it easier for him to listen to her—he didn't feel as criticized or defensive. After communicating her feelings, Sarah listened patiently and openly when Robert told her how he felt about the situation. He was able to feel her genuine interest in understanding him without being judgmental; this helped Robert express himself more freely. And they grew closer.

You may have observed certain problems with your stepchildren or family dynamics. Initially, your spouse may dismiss your insights, which can be discouraging. Make sure to pick a time that is good for both you and your partner to discuss your concerns. And when you do, take the time to understand your partner's perspective thoroughly before you insist on being understood yourself. Not only is this a more effective communication approach, but it will help build a sense of emotional safety and caring in your partner.

Points to Ponder

- Before you make your own case, make sure you understand everything your spouse is telling you. After sharing his or her perspective with you, your partner will know that you heard if you repeat it back (without adding your slant) and ask if you got it right.
- After your partner feels understood, it's your turn to share your thoughts and feelings. Allow each other to share perspectives.
- Make your love and commitment to each other the highest priority.

It can be hard to speak clearly and listen well if you are emotionally upset. If you find it difficult to stay calm and not to interrupt, try practicing a breathing exercise. You can do this while you are listening to your partner speak. Put one hand on your chest and the other hand on your lower belly. Clear your mind of all thoughts. Let your mind be empty, open, and ready to listen. At the same time, take slow breaths, making sure that when you inhale, your lower belly moves more than your chest. This breathing exercise will help you to breathe more deeply, allowing for full lung expansion, which supplies more oxygen to the body, and can help to calm your nervous system and your mind.

Jane and Stephen each brought children to their stepfamily, and they both worked hard at their jobs to support their stepfamily. They rarely argued about money; they made about the same salary and had each had two children. Neither of their spouses helped much financially, so they had a lot of responsibility on their shoulders. One night, Jane came home from work especially tired.

"I'm tired of working so hard and being exhausted all the time. I feel like I never catch up with anything," she said, craving for Stephen to put his arms around her and hold her tight.

Instead, Stephen shot back: "I never said you had to work so hard. Tell your boss you want to cut your hours!"

Jane was stunned. She had hoped for a little cuddle in his arms. She liked her job—it was just that she was in the mood for a little comfort, appreciation, and understanding. Things might have gone differently if Jane had told Stephen what she wanted; he wasn't a very good mind reader, especially when he was tired at the end of his day, too. As often happens in communications between loved ones, the listener focuses on his or her own reactions and feelings instead of empathizing with the speaker. In this case, Stephen heard Jane's words as a criticism of him as a provider and partner.

"My day wasn't exactly a cakewalk, you know. I had a grueling day—I was putting fires out from the minute I walked into my office. I'm going to watch TV and relax," Stephen responded gruffly.

What Jane really needed from Stephen was reassurance and a sense of caring about how she was feeling. If he had offered this to her for a few moments, most likely she would have felt better. She would then have been able to reciprocate. Especially when we are upset, it can help to take turns and to try to understand each other's feelings, one person at a time.

For example, it might have eased tensions if Stephen had said, "You have been working so hard, Jane. You make such a great contribution to our family in so many ways. I know how much you try to take care of so many things. Come here and let me hold you, honey. Is there anything I can do to help you feel better?" After this, if Stephen had then vented about his own day, chances are Jane would have been more supportive and understanding of his feelings.

Even more challenging and critical are conversations in which two people are expressing negative feelings toward each other. This is when it is especially hard to hear the other person out, rather than defending oneself. When you disagree, try to listen to each other's perspective with acceptance and as much understanding as possible. Even though you disagree, you can still accept each other's perspective and try to find a middle-ground solution or compromise. Once emotions are aired in an atmosphere of safety and caring, their intensity tends to diminish. When you both feel a certain degree of understanding and acceptance from each other, it is easier to work together toward compromises and practical solutions.

The expression on your face, your tone of voice, and the words you choose can help make or break your relationships. Many times people have better manners with strangers than they do with their family members at home. Being mindful about how you behave in your communication can help you build close relationships in a positive direction.

A Few Tips
- Try to be aware of your own biases, judgments, and opinions.
- Notice if you are focused on one person being right or the other being wrong.
- Give people the benefit of the doubt.
- Take time to make sure you understand the other person's point of view.
- Remember that things are rarely as clear-cut as we might think.
- Let your love be stronger than your need to be right or "win" the argument.

EXERCISES

1. Remember a time when you were positive you were right about something, only to realize later that it wasn't as simple as you had thought.

2. Try practicing Dr. Rosenberg's non-violent communication approach to making a request with your partner, children, or stepchildren below. Notice how it goes. Use the following outline to formulate your request before you make it.

A. Describe your observation.

_____

_____

_____

B. Identify your feeling.

_____

_____

_____

B. Explain the reason for your feeling in terms of your needs.

_____

_____

_____

C. State your request.

_____

_____

_____

Chapter Fifteen

Overbearing Stepfathers

"The demand to be loved is the greatest of all arrogant presumptions."
—FRIEDRICH NIETZSCHE

When Joanne married Gary, she felt so lucky. Her first husband wasn't around, and she had two sons. Gary was eager to be a father, and he quickly stepped into his new role. Joanne had grown up in a traditional family. Her mother had stayed home with the children, and her father worked. While her mother was happy in her homemaker role, she tended to leave the discipline to Joanne's father.

At the time Joanne met Gary she was struggling. She was juggling her job as a middle school teacher and raising her boys on her own. Their biological father had moved far away and only saw the boys a couple of times a year. When Joanne and Gary married, the children were nine and eleven years old. Gary was a military guy and believed in strict discipline. Joanne was used to her father handling the discipline, so she was relieved when Gary readily took on this role with the boys. Joanne's boys, however, were less enthralled with the new arrangement, and they rebelled. They didn't want to be disciplined by Gary. They had been cautiously open to having an adult male friend and seeing where it went, but Gary's overly zealous approach tainted their budding relationship. Joanne tried to support her husband, insisting the boys listen to Gary. Even when she felt his military background made him rigid at times, she still stood by him. That was what she believed was right. Deep down, she was afraid that if she openly disagreed with Gary, he would leave as her first husband had. The boys felt abandoned by their mother and grew resentful toward Gary (a good guy who just didn't understand the different dynamic in stepfamilies).

Eventually, things got so bad that Gary and Joanne sought counseling. They learned more about what works in stepfamilies, and Joanne discovered she was afraid to speak up when her opinion differed from Gary's. She thought her role was to please him and let him wear the pants in the family; that was how she was raised. She accepted things as they were without thinking about it. When Joanne felt uncomfortable with the way Gary treated her children, she would anxiously find a chore to occupy herself, avoiding confrontation. Eventually, through their open discussions in therapy, Joanne learned that Gary didn't want all of the responsibility for disciplining the boys but believed this was what she wanted from him. He really wanted to enjoy spending time with the boys, rather than being the disciplinarian.

Insidiously, we can slip into living out old roles and beliefs without even thinking about what we doing. Joanne and Gary were trying to please each other and meet what they thought were their partner's expectations. Their efforts were well intended but misplaced. More open communication and a little education helped them straighten out their misunderstandings. They didn't know that stepchildren don't take well to stepparents meting out the discipline—especially in the beginning. Joanne and Gary then renegotiated how they handled their family life together. Gary started focusing on nurturing his relationships with his stepsons. They went fishing, played baseball, and went to the movies together. Joanne started disciplining in her own way, and Gary backed her up. Eventually, things balanced out in their family.

It can be challenging for men who marry women with children to find their place in the family. Our preconceived notions about what it means to be a father, mother, husband, or wife don't fit neatly into the blended-family scenario. The particulars of your unique situation will determine the type of authority and participation you will have in your family.

Your role as a stepfather is going to depend on a number of factors:
- the age and the personality of the kids;
- the level of involvement of their father;
- whether their father is alive or deceased; and
- the type of relationship that you have with their mother.

Naturally, biological parents and their children have a bond that has been nurtured since infancy. The children were held, soothed, and fed, and they connected with their parents' eyes, voices, and smells. When you enter in children's lives as a stepparent, you don't have the built-in bond that biological parents enjoy.

As a stepfather, start by
- being interested and nurturing toward the children as the unique individuals they are;
- having conversations with them on subjects they choose; and
- leaving discipline to their biological parents (give your input behind the scenes to your spouse until you've established a solid bond, which may take years).

Movies, Books, and Fairy Tales

It's not unusual for a stepparent to feel left out of the special bonds in a spouse's biological family. Of course, we all know that the child-parent bond has a different quality than that of romantic partners, but we are not always rational beings. The parent-child relationship precedes the one you have with your new spouse and at times it can feel threatening, especially if you sometimes feel treated as a second-class citizen in your new family.

Books and movies give us visions of evil stepparents who plot to get rid of their stepchildren, going so far as hatching plans to kill them. Fortunately, most real-world stepparents don't have malicious intentions toward their stepchildren. To the contrary, stepparents are often inclined to bend over backwards to demonstrate their good intentions.

At the same time, some of these fictional tales have a basis in reality—there sometimes *is* a pea under the mattress. And children are going to be looking for that pea for a long time. You'll need to tread carefully with criticism, discipline, and any feelings of jealousy you may have. You are only human—you can't banish all feelings or thoughts of jealousy, competitiveness, or anger from your heart and mind.

Relationship Building with Your Stepchildren

- To build trust, be authentic and kind.
- Try to be present (not distracted) when you are with your stepchildren.
- Don't dwell on the past or the future—just experience the moment with them as it is, not as you think it should be.
- Accepting them as they are in a given moment can help them feel safer.
- Accept that earning their trust will come in fits and starts, and take time.
- You will take two steps back for every one step forward.
- Don't ever give up on them.

Stereotypes of the overbearing stepfather and wicked stepmother can haunt contemporary men and women trying to establish a decent and loving presence in the lives of their stepchildren. Most of us walk a different path than did the stepparents of our ancestors. And yet, the image of the monstrous, evil stepparent rears its head frequently in popular culture to this day. It can be hard for stepparents to express anger or other negative feelings without coming across like wicked stepmothers or evil stepfathers. Of course, it's natural to have a whole mix of emotions, but even more so than biological parents, you need to be discerning about when and how you share your feelings with the children.

Karen's stepdad had a rough start—the girl didn't like him because he wasn't her "real" dad. His presence meant that Karen's parents weren't getting back together. The sixteen-year-old was sarcastic and negative toward him. Her stepdad took her behavior personally and developed a caustic edge with her. At a certain point he decided he wouldn't give her a chance to hurt him anymore, so he did his best to stop caring. Their relationship remained contentious; the more time went by the harder it was for them to forgive each other.

Fathers can assume a natural leadership role with their children; but stepfathers often feel like they are starting from scratch with each new interaction. It's easy to react by withdrawing from your stepkids; but if you hang in there, you can become a source of support, encouragement, and love.

One of the best ways for stepparents to bond with their stepkids is to talk with them when they are in the mood. Have conversations in which you learn about what they are up to and what they are interested in. When you learn about their strengths and weaknesses as individuals, try to dwell on their strengths over their weak areas.

Common Frustrations
- Stepchildren determine the pace of the relationship.
- You can't force someone to open his or her heart to you.
- You have to earn the respect and acceptance of the kids, and this takes time.
- It's hard not to have more control over the process of establishing your role in your family.

Step Back and Go With the Flow
Brian was a counselor, and his stepson Jason had a drug problem. Audrey, Brian's wife, knew her son had a problem. Audrey and Brian

discussed Jason regularly, trying to figure out how best to help him. Jason's dad kept bailing him out of trouble. The biological parents and stepparents were all very involved and caring toward Jason. Nevertheless, Brian felt like he was walking on eggshells, never knowing when he'd say that one thing that would tweak a nerve in Audrey. He tried to be diplomatic and constructive in his comments, but sometimes, when he said something that seemed too hard or unsympathetic, Audrey would turn cold and defensive. At those moments, Brian felt like an outsider. Audrey would say that Jason was her son and that Brian just didn't understand. Audrey defended her son and then gave Brian the cold shoulder. For a little while, she would withhold information from him. Sometimes, Brian even felt jealous of the love and devotion Audrey bestowed on her son, even though this was also one of the things he loved about Audrey; feelings of jealousy often stem from fear of loss. Brian reminded himself that there was plenty of room in Audrey's heart for all of her loved ones.

Ultimately, Jason's parents decided how to handle the boy's problems. Brian didn't completely agree with their strategy, but no one asked him; his position was not unusual for a stepparent. Audrey felt good about being able to work with her ex-husband on behalf of their son. Jason seemed to like seeing his parents collaborate on his care. Sometimes as stepparents we do have to take a back seat and go with the flow, even if we don't completely agree with the decisions being made regarding our stepchildren. We are not in control—nor, in most cases, are we supposed to be.

Going with the flow, however, doesn't mean being a doormat. One time, I heard a popular counselor on the radio give advice to a stepfather. The man had called in regarding his three stepdaughters and his wife. He said his stepdaughters were slobs and wanted to know if he had the right to tell them to clean up after themselves. The widely respected counselor said, without hesitation, "No. You don't have the right. And don't tell me that you didn't know this was how they lived before you married their mother. It's sad that their mother would rather be their friend than teach them responsibility and discipline. But, no, you don't have the right." She then took the next caller.

In all fairness, she is an entertainer and has a limited time with each person. Nevertheless, I was shocked. Everyone in the household has rights, even stepparents. If, as a stepparent, you are coming from a judgmental place that the children "should" clean up after themselves, your family will probably be less receptive to you. But if you can communicate to your spouse, in a spirit of asking for respect and consideration, that you feel the personal boundaries in your home are being violated, you may be able to improve the situation for everyone over time. The way you communicate and the level of expectation for change can affect other people's reactions to you.

Advice for Stepdads

Following is a letter from and response to someone who wrote in to my advice column:

Dear Dr. Diana,

My husband is having problems with my sixteen-year-old daughter. I think she is angry that her dad and I are not getting back together, and my husband is getting the brunt of it. His presence in our house is a thorn in her side. She's sarcastic and negative toward him, and he is starting to withdraw from any kind of family activity. I try to explain to him that it's not personal, it's not really

A Summary of What Tends to Work for Stepfathers

- In the beginning, participate behind the scenes with your spouse by helping establish the boundaries, expectations, and values in the household while she handles the delivery of any kind of discipline or intervention.

- When an opportunity arises, let the kids know that you are not trying to replace their father, that you are committed to this marriage with their mother, and that this includes being married to the kids in a sense. This can be reassuring to children and encourage them to take the risk of caring about you.

- Try not to take the ups and downs personally; children often test stepparents to see what their

him she's mad at, but it's been getting harder for him to deal with it. We need some direction. Thank you.
—Floundering Mother and Wife

Dear Floundering,
It's common for a child to view her stepparent as representing the loss of her original family. When a child expresses her hurt by rejecting the new stepparent, it can be hard for the stepparent to not take it personally. The truth is that being a stepparent is usually more challenging than most people think it will be, just as parenting is more difficult than one anticipates. Stepparents can use the ups and downs of blended family life as an opportunity to grow their character. For example, for your husband to look past your daughter's anger and see it for what it is, he has to see beyond his own personal feelings. This doesn't mean that he should have to tolerate disrespectful treatment (ideally, you will insist that your daughter treat her stepdad with respect as another adult in the house).

character is and if they can be trusted.

- Model what you want to teach. If you practice good stress and anger management when things get rocky, the children will start feeling more comfortable opening up around you and counting on you as a reliable adult in their lives.

- Research indicates that the best thing a stepparent can do to bond with his or her stepkids is to talk with them. Have conversations with them about their activities and interests. Eventually (this is the key word), your attention and care for them will pay off.

Points of Interest

- The most common form of blended family is a mother and stepfather arrangement.

- Girls adapt less favorably than boys when custodial mothers remarry. Stepfathers disrupt the close ties many girls establish with their mothers in a single-parent family, and girls often react to the new marriage with sulky, resistant behavior.

148

EXERCISES

1. Think of something that you can do to help your stepchild or stepchildren feel welcome and at home in your house. Write it down. Check to see if your spouse agrees with your idea. If so, implement the idea while keeping low expectations for appreciation or recognition from the child.

_____

_____

_____

2. Next time you are having negative feelings toward one of your family members, pay attention to what you are thinking. How accurate and helpful are your thoughts? Are they making things worse, or are they constructive?

_____

_____

_____

3. Next time you are upset with one of your family members, try to be kind and gentle toward yourself while you work on balancing your focus with more positive thoughts about that individual. Write down any thoughts you may have on this matter.

_____

_____

_____

4. What kind of stepfather would you like to have? How would he treat your mom? What qualities would he have?

_____

_____

_____

_____

Chapter Sixteen

Wicked Stepmothers

*"Soul is not a thing, but a quality or a dimension of experiencing
life and ourselves. It has to do with depth, value, relatedness, heart, and
personal substance."*
—THOMAS MOORE

From the time I became a stepmother, my grandmother
encouraged me to be nice and decent to my stepchildren. You
see, my grandmother had a wicked stepmother. Grandma was a
Russian immigrant who came to the United States on a freighter
when she was seven years old. She was quarantined at Ellis Island
for three weeks because a family of lice had made a home in her hair
on the ride overseas. She didn't speak a word of English at the time.

When Grandma was two years old, she had been taken to live
with her grandmother because her own mother had died. Her
grandmother had seven other children of her own. At that same
time, Grandma's father left Russia for the United States, with the
plan to send for her later.

When Grandma arrived in the United States at the age of seven,
her father had remarried. Her stepmother was not very happy to share
her new husband with this beautiful little Russian immigrant. The

way Grandma told it, she had a traditional wicked stepmother, who maligned her to her father and continually tried to trip Grandma up. But Grandma was a tiny, tough, resilient Russian girl. She kept a low profile and determinedly made her way in the world.

Historically, stepmothers have a less than rosy image. The term *stepmother* is paired with negative events and the emotions of loss and pain. In the early days of our society, when a woman became a stepmother, it was because the biological mother had died. In fact, the prefix *step-* comes from a Latin word meaning "to grieve" or "to orphan." Furthermore, while the old stereotype of the "evil stepmother" is outdated, it's not out of people's minds. The "wicked stepmother" archetype is deeply implanted in our collective consciousness.

Stepparenting expert Lisa Cohn writes, "Often when women become stepmothers, they believe they should behave like Julie Andrews in the movie *The Sound of Music.* They expect instantly to be perfect caregivers and homemakers. Many assume that if they cook and care for stepkids daily, maybe even doing special things such as handcrafting clothing for the children, they'll soon be happily riding bikes with their stepchildren, singing and acting like one big happy family." Many stepmoms try too hard in the beginning, and it can set them up for rejection.

Try to step slowly into your new role. It can be helpful to sit down with your husband and talk about what your role with the children will be. If you try to assume a parental role with the kids too fast, they can resent you. You are best off encouraging their father's close involvement with his children as well as a respectful, cooperative relationship with his ex-wife. This will help the children feel less threatened by your presence in the family. Generally, our role as stepmothers or stepfathers is to be supportive to our spouses. If you try to build your relationships too fast, your family may feel like you are overstepping your bounds. Or you may experience what I did initially, when I heard that "I was too nice and that I might be trying too hard." Not scathing words by any means, but when you are just being yourself and that is the feedback, it can be confusing.

What I took away was that with my initial desire to connect with my stepdaughters they may have felt imposed on to develop a relationship at my pace, not theirs.

It's not unusual for stepchildren or their parents to reject stepparents' efforts. Indeed, parents' efforts are often rejected by their own children, but in the more tenuous step-relationship the bonds can feel more brittle or fragile. While the environment may be conducive to cultivating feeling unappreciated and resentful at times, it's important to keep things in perspective. As the woman of the household, you have a big impact on the emotional tone in your home. When your stepchildren come to visit, or when they live with you and your partner, your emotional thermostat helps set the climate of overall acceptance and love.

Stepmoms Can Be Peacemakers

It can be hard to fully understand the degree to which your husband may be willing to go to avoid conflict with his ex-spouse. Remember, for two people with children to get divorced, the marriage had to be pretty bad. Both adults have been through a lot to get to this point. At this stage, in the best scenario, the parents have had enough disagreement and want to get along as a protective measure for the children. Of course, most relatively healthy adults don't want their children hurt or in the middle of a war between their parents.

A biological father who is devoted to his children is often more willing to put his own feelings aside to accommodate his ex-wife than the stepmother is likely to be. For instance, most men say that last-minute schedule changes in which the children are coming to stay are not a big deal. But these kinds of changes are more stressful for stepmoms. This is in part because it often happens without their approval, and the woman is usually the one who cares for the majority of the children's needs in the home. Even when the dad is very involved, a woman is generally wired to tune into the feelings and needs of others, especially if she has strong, healthy maternal instincts. When the schedule is constantly changing, feeling resentful and out of control of her home life is a common reaction for stepmothers.

Blended families are fertile ground for egos, passionate opinions, and turf wars. Stepmoms can be peacemakers. We can start in our own homes. This is not about self-sacrifice. You must take care of yourself and your own needs as well; remember, when we are happier, we have more to give to those around us. But each individual in the household contributes to the culture of the home. How do you contribute to yours?

The Ever-Changing Schedule

Cindy was a stepmom without any children of her own. She loved her stepchildren but admitted that it had been a big adjustment for her. She complained that the biological mom imposed on the family by asking them to take the kids on any given day at the last minute. Her husband Dan would regularly tell her that the kids were on their way over on an off-schedule day, which made Cindy feel thrown off balance. Over time, Cindy developed resentment toward the ex-wife for her lack of consideration on schedule changes among other things and began giving her the cold shoulder.

After eight years of marriage, Cindy figured out it wasn't as simple as she'd previously thought. All that time, Cindy had thought it was a power struggle, with the ex-wife wanting to tell them how things were going to go with the kids. But it turned out that the changes were not as last minute as she had thought—they arose because her husband wasn't paying attention when he talked with his ex-wife. He had learned to zone out when talking with her, his way of avoiding conflict. But in the end, this created more conflict and negative feelings among various members of the family.

When Cindy and her husband discussed what was happening, Dan confessed to her that not only did he not pay close attention when talking with his ex-wife, but at other times he neglected to tell Cindy when his ex-wife did call and ask to change the schedule. He said that often his ex would call at the last minute to make an inconvenient change to the schedule, but within a short time, she would call back, having changed her mind and wanting to return to the formerly agreed upon schedule. If this sounds confusing, it is because it was. And Dan didn't want to risk causing distress or upset with Cindy if the schedule change was not going to materialize, so sometimes he didn't mention it. Regardless of whether he forgot to tell Cindy the schedule because he tuned out his ex-wife, or whether he just didn't want to rock the boat, it did.

Common Schedule-Change Challenges

- When changes are thrust upon the stepmom at the last minute, it's natural for her to feel a lack of control over her own life, left out, or disrespected.
- Stepparents often get left out of the loop when it comes to schedules and logistics conversations between husbands and their ex-wives (or wives and ex-husbands).
- Decisions are made that affect stepparents and children without consulting with them.

Points to Ponder

- Many stepparents have told me that they think that they have the clearest perspective of all the adults in a family because they are one step removed from all the past pain and drama in the divorced family.
- Stepparents can sometimes spot dysfunctional patterns of communication and behavior and if given a voice can steer the family toward healthier patterns of relating.
- Depending on the particulars of your situation, the degree of your involvement will differ.
- Including the stepparents in scheduling plans can be helpful toward cultivating a cooperative, cohesive family.
- When biological parents consistently make decisions that have a direct impact on the stepparent's life without consulting him or her, it can be a breeding ground for hurt, resentment, and anger.

It's Not Always What We Think

Judy had been married to Stephen for two years. She had two stepsons. Stephen's divorce from his ex-wife Nancy had been amicable. They remained quite friendly. Judy was a pretty thick-skinned person. She tended to see things realistically and was usually fairly optimistic. Two of Judy's strengths were her ability to love and be loved, and her kindness and compassion toward other people.

Over the first months of the new marriage, a pattern had developed. When Nancy dropped her boys off at dinnertime on Friday evenings, Judy invited Nancy to dinner. Nancy seemed sad and lonely. As a shy and quiet person, she seemed to be having difficulty moving on with her postdivorce life. Stephen and the boys seemed to enjoy Nancy staying for dinner on Friday nights, and Judy wanted everyone to be happy. Judy knew that Stephen felt some guilt toward the boys and Nancy for the divorce.

At first, Judy felt proud that they had created such an integrated blended family, but after about six months of this new routine, she found herself growing increasingly resentful. She noticed that she felt a little jealous of the friendship that seemed to have grown between Nancy and Stephen. She had developed a friendship of sorts with Nancy also, out of their mutual love for the boys; sometimes they also bonded by commiserating about what they thought to be Stephen's personal shortcomings. Understandably, Stephen didn't like that too much.

While it is unusual for first and second wives to be so friendly, it is becoming more common as women strive for ways to make the blended family unit work as well as possible. In order for that to happen, there has to be a certain degree of compatibility between the people as well as an adequate amount of mental health. Needless to say, when there are emotionally disturbed or unhealthy blended family members, the situation becomes much more complicated and difficult.

When Judy complained to her friends or family about her feelings of jealousy she would hear about how lucky she was that things were so amicable. She was reminded that things could be much worse. It's hard for people to understand what it's really like to share one's husband with another woman—especially when they have the special bond of sharing children together. Judy assumed that if she stopped inviting Nancy to stay for dinner, that the rest of the family would become angry with her. She found herself in the position of having created a situation that had grown uncomfortable but that she was afraid to change. She feared that her husband would think that she was selfish and unkind. When Judy finally got up the nerve to talk with Stephen about her feelings, his response startled her. He told her that it didn't matter to him and that it had never been all that comfortable for him. He had felt that if Judy was being so generous, he could at least try to extend himself also. Stephen thought that the boys were so young that they wouldn't notice the change all that much if was handled well. Judy's thinking had been inaccurate, and all of her feelings based on incorrect assumptions.

The following Friday night, Judy chose not to invite Nancy to stay for dinner. She told her a close enough version of the truth. "You know, Nancy, it's been a really busy week and we are just going to have a very early, quiet evening." She anticipated a hurt, disappointed look from Nancy. But instead, Nancy took it well, and confided that she welcomed a quiet evening at home at herself. She said that she hadn't wanted the children to think that she didn't want to be with them!

Clearly, this worked out well. But even if it hadn't, it was important that Judy consider her own needs as much as the others in the family.

It's also important not to mind-read. Gut feelings are not always right. Just recently, our cat Patsy got outside at nighttime. And as we were walking around looking for her, I told my husband with anguish and certainty in my voice, "I have a bad feeling about this. I think she is gone. I can feel it." A short while later, when our kitty came walking up to us, my husband turned it into a learning moment; he said that he hoped I would realize that when I feel or sense something, while I may be right a lot, there are times that I am not. And it's important that we not take action or react too strongly until we have the facts.

Points to Ponder

- Being a stepmom is not a sprint; it is a long-distance marathon.
- Being a stepmother provides an unending opportunity to work on one's own character and perspective.
- Being a martyr or enduring extreme self-sacrifice is not usually necessary or advised for the health of long-term relationships.
- The most challenging relationships in stepfamilies tend to be between stepmothers and stepdaughters.
- Women who become stepparents report having more difficulty coping with their role than men.
- Girls have an especially difficult time adjusting to stepmothers, although they tend to find adjusting to stepfathers challenging as well.
- Kids often fear betraying their mother if they accept love from their stepmother.
- Noncustodial mothers are more likely to maintain contact with children than noncustodial fathers, and frequent visits between mother and daughter are likely to cause increased conflict between stepmother and stepdaughter.
- Even when the biological mother is the noncustodial parent, children generally tend to be more emotionally attached to their mother than their father, which can make it more difficult to bond with their stepmother.

Exercises

1. Remember a time when you had a negative understanding or view of a situation and then later found out that you were incorrect, things were not as bad as you initially perceived them to be.

_____

_____

_____

_____

_____

_____

2. Think of a stepchild or blended family member whom you find particularly challenging. Try imagining things in reverse: if you were that person and that person were you, how would you want them to treat you? Write it down.

_____

_____

_____

_____

_____

_____

3. Now write about each of your stepkids and biological children individually. Writing from their perspective, how do you think that they want you to treat them and relate with them? Share your writing with your partner and get input.

_____

_____

_____

_____

_____

_____

4. Next time you are having negative feelings toward one of your family members, pay attention to what you are thinking. How accurate and helpful are your thoughts? Are they making things worse, or are they constructive?

_____

_____

_____

_____

_____

_____

_____

_____

5. Next time you are upset with one of your family members, try to be kind and gentle toward yourself while you work on balancing your focus with more positive thoughts about that individual. Write down any thoughts you have about this.

_____

_____

_____

_____

_____

_____

_____

_____

_____

_____

_____

_____

_____

6. What kind of stepmother would you like to have? How would she treat your father? What qualities would she have?

_____

_____

_____

_____

_____

_____

_____

_____

_____

_____

_____

Chapter Seventeen

Encouragement for the Road Weary

"You know quite well, deep within you, that there is only a single magic, a single power, a single salvation . . . and that is called loving. Well, then, love your suffering. Do not resist it. Do not flee from it. It is your aversion that hurts nothing else."
—HERMAN HESSE

In the 2007 film *Juno,* Juno and her stepmother share a mutual animosity toward one other. For example, several times throughout the movie, Juno empties the remains of her large, bizarre, blue-colored soda into a special urn that belongs to her stepmother. Juno denies that she did it, although it is obvious to her stepmother that Juno is the culprit. Naturally, Juno's stepmother is irritated and silently sullen about Juno's defiling her coveted, decorative, ceramic jar. The two have a cantankerous relationship but when the chips are down, her stepmother is there for her. At the young age of sixteen, Juno gets pregnant. Since her biological mother died several years prior, Juno only has her father and stepmother for guidance and support. One of the most touching parts of the movie for me was watching Juno's stepmother come through for her. Despite Juno's prior hostility, in Juno's time of need the stepmother is there for her. She doesn't allow Juno's belligerent attitude to diminish her steady presence and support. The stepmother's acceptance and commitment to Juno is admirable and touching.

Parents become ingrained in the fabric of a child's life through years of experiences and memories woven together. It doesn't happen overnight. Children hurt their parents' feelings in various ways all the time. When we love and care about another human being so much, getting hurt from time to time goes with the territory. It's how these injuries are repaired that is the key to maintaining the goodwill in these relationships. In the film, when an opportunity to be there for Juno arises, the stepmother's compassion for Juno takes over and helps repair and build their relationship. At the end of the film, when her stepmother is with her in the delivery room, one gets the sense that Juno and her stepmother are bonding at a new level. The film doesn't spell out how Juno's stepmom let go of any hard feelings she may have had toward Juno. But one gets the feeling that the stepmom's love and compassion for Juno superseded any negativity they'd had in the past.

Points to Ponder

- As a stepparent in a blended family, you'll have many opportunities to practice forgiveness.
- Harboring feelings of anger or resentment diminishes our energy and vitality.
- There are many reasons to learn the art of forgiveness.
- Forgiveness is good for your physical and emotional health.
- With forgiveness comes an acceptance and peace in the here and now.

So, how do you handle and recover from being hurt by one of your stepchildren or other blended-family members?

Lola's son was a young adult living on his own when she married Tariq. His two daughters were six years old and eleven years old.

Lola had always wanted to have a daughter, and she dug in right away, working at cultivating a close relationship with the girls. Six-year-old Sophia was a daddy's girl and more open to the relationship with Lola. She was glad to see her father happy and enjoyed her time when she was with her dad and Lola. Her older sister Jasmine was very close with her mother. While Jasmine didn't mind Lola, she kept a distance and tended to push her away if she tried to get too close. Their relationship had its moments where they felt warm and connected, and Lola always tried to build on those. She knew that Jasmine worried about her mother, who had never remarried. She assumed that as a loving, loyal daughter, Jasmine didn't want to hurt her mother by being too close or happy with her stepmother. Lola tried hard over the years to not take it personally when she felt pushed away by Jasmine.

Many years later, Jasmine moved away to attend a culinary school. Her father and Lola went to visit her at school. One evening on that trip, Lola and Jasmine were having a particularly warm moment and Lola turned to Jasmine and told her, "I love you and your sister so much. You are the closest things to having my own daughters that I'll ever have." To which Jasmine coldly replied, "Well, that's fine. As long as you don't mind that we don't feel the same way."

Lola later described in her counseling session that she felt like someone had kung-fu kicked her in the heart. She swallowed hard and tried to let it roll off her back, as she was accustomed to doing. But as the evening wore on, it was stuck in her throat like a piece of stale bread that just wouldn't go down. That very night, she told her husband about what had happened and how hurt she felt. As usual, he was sympathetic. He felt saddened to hear what had happened. He tried to reassure his wife that his daughter hadn't meant anything personal by it, that she just had leftover issues with her parents' divorce. It's a hard position to be in: seeing your beloved hurt by one of the children that you love and feel protective of. Complete the package with the guilt that many parents feel regarding putting their children through a divorce—talk about being in the middle! Lola told her husband that she didn't think that she could let it go this time, that she was going to need to find a way to bring it up with her stepdaughter.

The following day was going to be a special treat. Jasmine had been a competitive ice skater as a child. An international ice-skating competition was taking place the next day. Lola had bought tickets for the three of them to attend the event. She had also made reservations at a restaurant with a world-famous chef—she thought that it would be exciting for Jasmine. Lola asked Jasmine to meet them outside the skating facility at 2:00 p.m., as the competition started at 2:30. Jasmine arrived at 2:28, so they almost missed the beginning of the skating. Lola felt disrespected. She was already feeling hurt from the night before and after listening to Jasmine's flimsy excuses, Lola began to feel furious. She felt unfairly treated and that Jasmine was doing it on purpose.

During the skating competition, when Jasmine turned to Lola and apologized to her again (Jasmine probably couldn't help but notice that Lola was angry), Lola didn't accept the apology. Instead, she decided to bring up the night before. Perhaps, it took being angry for Lola to stand up for herself and bring up a difficult topic, but her timing was not ideal. Lola was brimming with indignant anger; her intensity was palpable.

"You hurt my feelings last night when I told you that I love you and your sister and that you are both like daughters to me, and you told me that it was okay as long as I understood that you both didn't feel the same way! That was so unnecessary to say, even if it's true. It was mean and really hurt my feelings. You do that every once in a while, where out of the blue you are mean to me. Maybe when we start getting too close for comfort, you need to push me away. That's okay. But I won't accept this kind of treatment from you anymore. I don't deserve it."

"You are totally out of line," proclaimed Jasmine.

Lola pleaded with Jasmine, "Please, just try to hear my feelings. I feel hurt by what you said. I need you to be more careful in how you talk to me."

"I'm out of here," said Jasmine. And with that, she turned on her heel and was lost in the crowd.

"What just happened?" asked Jasmine's father.

Lola was shocked and shaking. She tried to explain to Tariq what had happened.

He shook his head. "Probably not the best timing, but I understand she really pushed your buttons. I'm sorry. She'll be back."

But she didn't come back. Lola and Tariq stayed for the rest of the skating competition, watching and waiting for Jasmine to return. They were shocked when she didn't. As Lola and Tariq walked out of the skating arena, Tariq told Lola his true feelings.

"It's never a good idea to try to talk about things when you are that angry."

Lola balked at that. "I wasn't that angry, I was mostly hurt."

"I know you were hurt, honey, but you must admit that you were angry too. You have every right to be hurt and angry. It's understandable, with how she treated you. But it's never a good idea to bring these things up in anger. And the timing was bad. I'm not justifying her actions, but it's important to recognize how you played a part in this."

Lola grew quiet as they walked along the street to their car. And then Tariq's phone rang. It was Jasmine, calling to complain about how her stepmom had treated her. Tariq was smash bang right in the middle of two upset women for whom he had great love. He played referee to some degree, trying to get each one to see her part in the episode. Eventually things calmed down, and Jasmine joined them for dinner. They talked for a long time—until the manager began putting chairs on the table so they could clean the floors. It was a heart-to-heart discussion between Jasmine and Lola; Tariq ran interference when necessary, but mostly he was quiet and let the women talk. Lola had decided that she needed to "fall on her own sword" and assume as much responsibility as she could. She apologized to Jasmine for speaking to her in anger and upsetting her. She acknowledged that the timing was bad. Jasmine had calmed down a lot. She told Lola that she didn't want to hurt her feelings, that she loved her. Lola could see the tears in her eyes and the remorse in her face. Lola asked her what was going on. She pointed out that this was a pattern. Why did that happen? Why did Jasmine sometimes lash out at her right when they were bonding? Jasmine thought about it and said that she didn't completely understand it herself. She remembered times when Lola was trying to be loving but it ended up hurting Jasmine—like when Lola told Jasmine that she wished she'd known her as a little girl because she must have been just adorable. Jasmine said that she heard it as Lola wishing that her parents had divorced earlier. Lola reassured Jasmine that was not what she had meant. But she was beginning to understand that her desire to be loving and close was sometimes painful to her stepdaughter. That was the last thing that she wanted. She suggested that in order to avoid hurting Jasmine, she would pull back and let Jasmine come to her when she wanted to connect. Jasmine thought that would be okay. She had a very close relationship with her mom and her dad, and she didn't really need much from Lola. She was just glad that her Dad was happy. So that's how they left it.

Admittedly there was a strain between them after that. But they both understood each other better. They had love for each other, but their relationship took a unique shape. Lola had to work at not taking Jasmine's coolness personally—she had to accept that their relationship might have certain limitations. Just because it wasn't going to be what Lola had wanted, which was for her to be a "second mother" figure, didn't mean that Jasmine was wrong for not wanting that. Over time, Jasmine and Lola accepted their differences and focused on their shared love for the other family members. In the end, that in itself created a new kind of bond—while they both tried hard not to hurt each other going forward. How do you guard your heart while still keeping it open? Ideally, you learn from your experiences without closing your heart or holding grudges.

Forgiving When You Feel Treated Unfairly or Justified in Your Anger, Hurt, or Resentment

- Try to understand and accept the other person's perspective as equally valid as your own.
- Have empathy for the person you feel hurt by.
- Challenge the rigid rules that you have for other people's behavior.
- If you get any kind of apology, accept it, especially if it's heartfelt.
- Focus on the good in your life rather than dwelling on a painful experience.
- It's easier to forgive when you don't allow negative experiences of the past to ruin your today.

Forgiving for the Sake of Love

Matthew had been a holy terror since he was two and a half years old. His parents split up when we was ten years old. Matthew took the divorce quite hard, and dropping his friends and his grades. His parents were both pretty distracted with postdivorce concerns of their own, and Matthew slipped a bit under the radar. It wasn't until Matthew began getting in trouble in middle school that his parents took any real notice. Both parents were called to the principal's office and told that if they wanted to keep Matthew in school, they had to get him some counseling. It was a rocky road for a while, but with some help, Matthew began to pull out of the ditch that he had built for himself.

By the time Matthew's mom Martha remarried to a man named Arlo, Matthew was getting decent grades and had an after-school job. He continued to be temperamental but at a milder pitch. As an only child, Matthew wasn't too keen on the idea of sharing his mom with another man besides his father. From the start, Matthew tried to create problems between his mom and Arlo, insisting that his mom side with him over her husband. For example, Arlo and Matthew had started wrestling every once and a while. Matthew was in wrestling at school, and Arlo thought it was a good activity for them to share. Arlo didn't always let Matthew win, because he wanted to challenge him. From time to time, Matthew would go to his mother and pretend to be hurt or complain that Arlo was unnecessarily rough with him. Arlo was very careful and felt quite defensive when his wife would approach him regarding this issue. Eventually, he had to stop wrestling with Matthew.

His mom loved her son of course, and always tried to see the best in him. It's partly what parents are supposed to do, right? We try to bring out the best in our kids, and in order to cultivate the best, we must look for it.

Over time, after lots of arguing, Martha and Arlo began to see eye to eye and recognize Matthew's manipulations. Martha began standing up to Matthew on behalf of her husband, insisting that Matthew behave appropriately. Things improved but even so, there remained a subtle, ever-present undercurrent of resentment and hostility toward Arlo. Even though his stepfather tried hard to win him over with kindness and friendship, Matthew's icy shell did not thaw. It was really hard on Martha, who felt like she was in the middle. Her son needed her, especially with all of his problems. And she loved Arlo and didn't want him to be hurt or angry. Arlo was frustrated that he couldn't make it better and angry because he felt unfairly treated by Matthew. His negativity toward his stepson only made things worse for his wife, his stepson, and himself.

One day, when Arlo was talking with a close friend about the situation, the friend suggested that he needed to forgive Matthew for the ongoing difficulties in their family. Arlo recognized that he was harboring resentments, but he didn't want to be a pansy and forgive and forget only to be hurt again. Finally one day, inspired by his love for Martha, he hit on it—don't forget, but forgive. It was better for his marriage if he could find forgiveness in his heart for his stepson. While Matthew was not someone that Arlo would chose to be around very much, he made a conscious decision to forgive and accept his stepson as best as he could for the sake of Martha. And it worked. His heart softened enough that his anger didn't make things worse. Matthew had learned not to mess with Arlo, and they managed to find a neutral coexistence that worked.

Points to Ponder
- Forgiving doesn't mean forgetting.
- Forgiving doesn't mean allowing the offensive behavior to continue.
- Forgiving demonstrates a deep compassion for others.
- Forgiving softens and stretches our hearts.
- Forgiving is good for our health and relationships.

Learning Opportunities
When Leanne married her husband Charlie, she was childless and he had two little boys from his previous marriage. She was eager to love her stepsons and improve their lives in any way that she could. Charlie was an easygoing guy who didn't set many rules for, assign many chores to, or impose much discipline on his boys. He was just glad to have a peaceful and for the most part happy household.

Leanne found it difficult to adjust to the way Charlie ran his household. She thought the boys were lazy and messy. She'd ask for help to no avail. As you might expect, after a while she got tired of nagging and would pick up the house herself. But as it goes, over time feelings of resentment would build up and eventually Leanne would blow a fuse when her family was least expecting it. Charlie was protective of his boys—he didn't want them to be hurt. When he reprimanded her in front of the boys, it was a defining moment for Leanne. Charlie had picked his sons over her. Needless to say, the boys took note of their father's position and ignored Leanne's requests for help even more.

As commonly happens, Charlie and Leanne had to sort out how to handle the children in a way that wasn't destructive to their marriage. Charlie drew the line at Leanne losing her temper with the boys, and her line was Charlie reprimanding her in front of the boys.

Leanne was an engineer. She was very analytical and had never considered herself to be an emotional person. Generally, she didn't pay much attention to what she was feeling most of the time. In order to control her temper, Leanne had to become aware of when her negative feelings were building. That way she could do or say something about it before the dam burst; She could talk with Charlie and the boys about problems before they became too big. Their family life improved. But the template had been somewhat set early on in their marriage and the boys continued to have a power struggle with Leanne, often putting their dad in the middle.

At times, Leanne felt frustrated with some of the challenges that came with her stepfamily. Even though things had improved, there was still this resentment pea under the mattress that wouldn't go away. It wasn't until Leanne and Charlie had a biological child of their own that her resentment faded. She came to appreciate the value of all that she had learned with her stepsons—about controlling her temper and developing more sensitivity to her own emotions and those of others.

She could better understand her husband's protective instinct toward his boys. And she realized that being a stepmother in her situation had helped her grow in ways that would make her a more even-tempered mother. If it hadn't been for her stepfamily, she would have had to learn the same lessons with her own child; instead she started motherhood managing her temperament better.

True forgiveness is appreciating the offending parties for helping you learn lessons that you needed to learn. It helps to

- acknowledge the role you are playing in your own suffering;
- embrace the lessons inherent in the challenges that you are presented with;
- begin to heal your pain;
- accept and work with your own shortcomings, so that you can then better accept that everyone has shortcomings; and
- recognize that there is good in everyone—we just have to look for it.

"Resentment, one of the core elements of un-forgiveness, is like carrying around a red-hot rock with the intention of someday throwing it back at the one who hurt you. It tires us and burns us. Who wouldn't want simply to let the rock fall to the ground?"
—EVERETT WORTHINGTON

Forgiveness Will Set You Free

Sometimes in stepfamilies, compromises are hard to come by and someone is asked to adapt to the group; this is often the stepparent—the new kid on the block. Whenever you can, try to guard against developing resentments and building up layers of negative feelings. Letting go of resistance doesn't mean that you deny your feelings or become a doormat. There are times when you'll need to draw a line in the sand. Everyone has different boundaries for what they can tolerate and what they can't. Ideally, you and your spouse and your stepchildren can discuss issues respectfully and search for compromises together. But when there are longstanding issues in the family that you cannot change or control, you will be better off if you can learn to accept that you cannot change the situation.

You've probably heard the expression, "Do your best and forget the rest." There is some real wisdom in recognizing what you cannot change in other people and accepting that fact, and then focusing your energy on what you can change—your own thoughts and reaction patterns, for example. You may not be able to change the way you feel about a particular situation, but it's important to have the self-awareness to know what you are experiencing inside, and then choose how you are going to respond. So, do your best to be realistic about what changes you can effect and what you need to become accustomed to—you will feel lighter and happier if you don't harp or dwell on the unchanging underbelly of your family. Your partner is likely to appreciate your acceptance also.

Tips for Stepparents
- Try to keep your thoughts free of negativity (prejudice, superstition, and delusion).

- Try to keep your mind focused on constructive and truthful attitudes and actions.
- Try to avoid speaking or listening to unproductive negative talk about other people, and try to speak kindly of other people instead. (It feels better!)
- Whenever you can, behave in kind, peaceful, and compassionate ways.
- Do your best to come from good intentions in all your endeavors.
- Take quiet time every day to concentrate on the stillness within you, the oneness of all life; acknowledge the divine light that exists in all human beings.

EXERCISES

1. Think about a situation that is aggravating you. Ask yourself what kind of lesson is presenting itself to you here.

_____

_____

_____

_____

_____

_____

_____

_____

2. Once you recognize what the lesson is, find a solution—a new approach to handle the situation so that it is less aggravating to you.

_____

_____

_____

_____

_____

_____

_____

_____

3. Pick the person in your blended family that you find most challenging to deal with. Repeat the following thoughts to yourself:

"Just like me, this person wants some happiness for his/her life."

"Just like me, this person wants to avoid suffering in his/her life."

"Just like me, this person has experienced sadness, loneliness, and despair."

"Just like me, this person wants to fulfill his/her desires and needs."

"Just like me, this person is learning about life."

Chapter Eighteen

Putting It All Together

"The truth you believe in and cling to makes you unable to hear anything new."
—PEMA CHODRON

Historically, stepparents have been a minority, so to speak. But in the United States today, stepparents outnumber biological parents. And with our collective experience, we understand much more about what's involved with being a stepparent. If we choose to, we can have a distinct role to play in stepfamilies. It helps if we understand and accept the inherent boundaries and issues involved in order to make the most of our situation; some of these have been highlighted in this book.

As stepparents, it's helpful to have realistic expectations for our relationships—especially when it comes to our stepchildren. As a woman without children of her own, when I married, part of what I was looking for was a family. Thankfully, I felt a natural rapport with my stepdaughters and anticipated accurately that we would enrich one another's lives. While many stepchildren don't need another parent, most can benefit from another committed and caring adult in their lives.

Along the way, I've learned so much. One of the biggest lessons is to take responsibility for my own happiness and well-being so that I can bring my best self into my family. Rather than expecting them to help me feel good, I've gotten better at accepting things as they come and recognizing what I can and cannot control. What I can control is my own attitude and resiliency. I can choose kindness, patience, and love whenever possible, and that in turn makes me stronger and happier. As it is with all of us, my personal best changes from moment to moment, depending on time of day, sleep, diet, stress, type of situation, and buttons being pushed.

No matter what, the experience of being a stepparent can help you deepen and strengthen your character. At the end of day, we become who we think we are, and our lives and relationships are what we make of them. We must turn to ourselves and then to our partners to work together to make the most of our lives.

In all honesty, sometimes I've felt like an outsider in my stepfamily. At those times, I am acutely aware of the difference between my relationship with my stepdaughters and their relationship with my husband, their biological father. That makes me wish I had been a part of their lives from the beginning so we would all have a deeper sense of belonging together. It can be painful.

Sometimes the smallest gesture or word can trigger these kinds of feelings. And of course if I dwell on them, I can think of more and more supporting evidence for the negative tone. And then I remember the old adage that whatever we focus on expands. We can choose our perspective. So, for a moment, I pretend that my stepdaughters are actually my biological daughters together with my husband. And I feel what that would be like. Then I realize that even if that were the case, my husband would still have a special connection with each of his daughters, which is different than the bond between mothers and daughters. It really doesn't have anything to do with me belonging or not. My perspective then broadens to a wider lens, and I know I have my place in my family. My stepdaughters know that I love them and that I am here for them if they need me. My husband and I have created a solid foundation that they can count on as a home base as they explore the world. And their mother has done the same with her husband. We have a successful blended family because we have well-adjusted, healthy children and happy marriages. In this book, I have tried to share with you some ideas about what has worked for other people, as well as for my family and me.

If we can grow and apply our strengths on our journey, we can become good role models and reliable, valuable family members. As stepparents we enter into an already formed family (albeit broken to various degrees), and we hope to be incorporated in a meaningful way. And dare I say that we hope to love and be loved? Most of us enter into our blended families with a generous heart and determined idealism.

A Few Points to Ponder

- It's normal for it to take years for a stepfamily or blended family to get to a place where all the individuals really feel like family.
- While it may take years to establish a cohesive blended family, it is possible.
- Stepparents can be effective and valued rudders for a family vessel that was cut loose in choppy waters.
- When we have a realistic idea of what to expect in our role as stepparent, it's easier to go the distance.

At the end of the day, being a stepparent is likely to trigger our deepest attachment issues. Children and parents who have gone through divorce are also dealing with concerns about the stability and reliability of their relationships. We all want to feel a sense of acceptance and belonging, especially in our families; it's part of the human condition. We are wired to want connection as part of the survival of the fittest. As human beings, without tusks, fangs, or claws, we die in isolation—physically and emotionally. A stepparents can feel like an outsider in his or her new family—being the new kid on the block in a stepfamily is not for the faint of heart.

To be successful, the couple must work collaboratively on solidifying their marriage and presenting a unified presence to the children; this can help create a secure foundation for the new family unit. The extra work required to develop a harmonious blended family can help you and your spouse build an even deeper, stronger relationship.

A Few Points to Ponder

- Check in regularly with your partner about how things are going.
- Ask for what you need from your partner. Don't expect him or her to read your mind.
- Find out what specific needs your partner has for you in your family.
- Be mindful to look for what's right in what the other says, rather than what is wrong.
- Put yourself in the other person's shoes to understand his or her perspective.
- Partners especially need to feel a safe emotional harbor with each other.

As with anything, a relationship is what you make of it. Even in the most challenging of situations, I want to encourage you to look deep within yourself, stretch your heart, and give others the benefit of the doubt until it's utterly stupid to do so. Even the most happily married couples find themselves challenged by the psychological complexities of living in a stepfamily or blended family.

There are no simple solutions. Each person has his or her own perspective and needs; but at the root of it, we are all looking to be accepted, understood, and loved. We band in families out of a need to belong—it is a deep survival mechanism. Human beings survive better in groups; we die in isolation.

Being a stepparent means putting yourself in a vulnerable position. You are stepping into a preexisting family and trying to create healthy, effective relationships in a system that may not always welcome you. Stepchildren can be conflicted about letting the relationship develop naturally; they may feel they are betraying their other biological parent, or see the stepparent as a painful reminder of what they've lost.

But the main point in this book is that being a stepparent is a great opportunity for personal development and learning how to create secure, loving, emotional bonds. You may not be able to control the situation or people's responses to you, but you are in charge of yourself. For example, we know that being emotionally present with kind intentions and responsiveness is essential to love and loving. And at the end of the day, if there is nothing that you can do to positively affect a situation, you can focus on being the best person possible. Not only is this a good role model for every person involved in the family, it will also assist you in your own well-being. Sometimes, the only thing that we can do is to tend to our own happiness and marriage.

A Few More Points to Ponder

- Your primary responsibility is to your spouse and your marriage.
- Cultivating and maintaining a healthy, loving marriage is beneficial to your stepchildren.
- As a human being, you have an immense capacity for love, acts of kindness, and personal growth.
- Being a stepparent provides tremendous inspiration for stretching your heart, acquiring perspective, making the most of what you can control, and letting go of the rest.
- You can apply your own strengths and experience to the stepfamily in ways that increase the well-being of all concerned.

Naturally, we all see the world through our own filters or perspectives. If you can be aware of your thoughts and emotions, you will be better equipped to choose how you respond, instead of having knee-jerk reactions. Being a stepparent has inspired me to have better self-regulation. Everyone has a right to his or her view. In our relationships, we get along better when we are aware of our perspective bias and don't insist that others share our view. We'd like people to understand us, but that doesn't mean everyone else has to agree with us. The most satisfying relationships are those in which people listen to each other respectfully and with empathy. Every relationship, every family, has problems that don't ever go away. It's how we deal with each other that is the crucial factor in how well we get along. For example, biological parents and stepparents form a primary unit that becomes the foundation of a stepfamily. Rituals and understandings of the "first" family that predate the blended family can trigger discomfort in a stepparent. Ideally, we can adjust to some of the family's preexisting traditions as well as creating some new ones together. It's important to remember that the biological parent (your spouse) is dealing with frustrations such as having less time to spend with his or her children. Family traditions and rituals can help create a sense of familiarity and stability during a time of transition and upheaval.

There will be many moments of conflicting needs within the family. One person feels disturbed or doesn't like something and brings it up with his or her mom or dad or significant other. Someone reacts defensively—perhaps feeling confused and criticized for doing what he or she has always done. The way the couple handles these moments will shape the culture of the new family. When the couple can listen to one another with an emphasis on mutual understanding and empathy, they can work almost anything out. And then they can teach this method to the children in the family.

If your stepchildren are open to the idea, develop your own relationship with them apart from their relationship with their mom or dad; it can be rewarding. Try and set aside some special time in which you and the stepchild can interact alone. Spending time with just the two of you can help you get to know each other as individuals. Make no doubt about it; you are a pivotal person in that child's life.

Creating a secure bond with your spouse and the children will help build hope and resiliency in your new family unit. Then you can start creating your own positive memories and history. The challenges of being a stepparent can offer you a chance to let go of a limited view of reality. When we let go of our notions of how things should be—especially when we can't change them anyway—we free up space for acceptance and love.

A Few Points to Ponder
- It's important to remember that the children didn't choose the situation—they are along for the ride.
- They will require sensitivity and patience while they adapt.
- They will grow up and move on to live their own lives.
- Tending to your marriage is a top priority, as it is the bedrock of the family as well as your future.

This book is offered as a guide through the challenges and joys of stepparenting, based on positive psychology and practical philosophy. We are all works in progress. Nobody does it perfectly. (Should I have said this earlier?) But we can and should strive always to give the best of ourselves, for the sake of both our own well-being and that of our loved ones. Our personal best will vary from day to day, but when it is fueled by the desire for love, growth, and connection, it can cultivate great hope.

Here's hoping that by reading this book, you've gained
- a sense of realistic expectations;
- some research-based tools for building healthy, loving relationships with partners and stepchildren;
- attitude adjustment strategies;
- understanding of the power of self-awareness and accountability—knowing what you are contributing to the positive or negative dynamics in your family; and
- inspiration to try and give your best because you can make a difference with your presence.

Thank you for reading my book, and may you find the rewards of being a stepparent far outweigh any difficulties you encounter.

Bibliography

Arhons, Constance. *The Good Divorce.* New York: HarperCollins, 1995.

———. *We're Still Family.* New York: HarperCollins, 2002.

Baxter, Leslie A., Dawn O. Braithwaite, and John H. Nicholson. "Turning Points in the Development of Blended Families." *Journal of Social and Personal Relationships* 16, no. 3 (1999): 291–313.

Bowlby, John. *A Secure Base: Parent-Child Attachment and Healthy Human Development.* New York: Basic Books, 1988.

Bray, James, and John Kelly. *Stepfamilies.* New York: Broadway Books, 1999.

Childre, Doc Lew, Howard Martin, and Donna Beech. *The Heart Math Solution: The Institute of HeartMath's Revolutionary Program for Engaging the Power of the Heart's Intelligence.* New York: HarperCollins, 2000.

Chodron, Pema. *Start Where You Are: A Guide to Compassionate Living.* Boston: Shambhala Audio, 2008.

Chopra, Deepak. *The Path to Love: Renewing the Power of Spirit in Your Life.* New York: Harmony Books, 1997.

Deal, Ron. *The Smart Stepfamily: Seven Steps to a Healthy Family.* Grand Rapids: Bethany House, 2006.

Fanning, Patrick, and Matthew McKay, eds. *The Family Guide to Emotional Wellness: Proven Self-Help Techniques and Exercises for Dealing with Common Problems and Building Crucial Life Skills.* Oakland: New Harbinger, 2000.

Fredrickson, Barbara L. *Positivity: Groundbreaking Research Reveals How to Embrace the Hidden Strength of Positive Emotions, Overcome Negativity, and Thrive.* New York: Crown Publishers, 2009.

Gable, Shelly L., Gian C. Gonzaga, and Amy Strachman. "Will You Be There for Me When Things Go Right? Supportive Responses to Positive Event Disclosures." *Journal of Personality and Social Psychology* 91, no. 5 (2006): 904-17.

Gable, Shelly L., and Jonathan Haidt. "What (and Why) is Positive Psychology?" *Review of General Psychology* 9, no. 3 (2005): 103–10.

Gable, Shelly L., and Jennifer G. La Guardia. "Positive Processes in Close Relationships across Time, Partners, and Context: A Multilevel Approach." In *Oxford Handbook of Methods in Positive Psychology,* edited by Anthony D. Ong and Manfred H, M. van Dulmen, 576–90. New York: Oxford University Press, 2007.

Ganong, Lawrence, Marilyn Coleman, Mark Fine, and Patricia Martin. "Stepparents' Affinity-Seeking and Affinity-Maintaining Strategies with Stepchildren." *Journal of Family Issues* 20, no. 3 (1999): 299–327.

Garmezy, N. "Resilience in Children's Adaptation to Negative Life Events and Stressed Environments." *Pediatric Annals* 20 (1991): 459–66;

Glick, Paul C. "Remarried Families, Stepfamilies, and Stepchildren: A Brief Demographic Profile." *Family Relations* 38 (1989): 24–28.

Glick, Paul C., and Sung-Ling Lin. "Remarriage after Divorce: Recent Changes and Demographic Variation." *Sociological Perspectives* 30, no. 2 (1987): 162–67.

Goleman, Daniel. *Emotional Intelligence: Why It Can Matter More Than IQ.* New York: Bantam Books, 1997.

Bibliography

Gottman, John, and Robert Levenson. "A Two-Factor Model for Predicting When a Couple Will Divorce: Exploratory Analyses Using 14-Year Longitudinal Data." *Family Process* 41, no. 1 (2002), 83–96.

Gottman, John, Robert Levenson, and Erica Woodin. "Facial Expressions During Marital Conflict." *Journal of Family Communication* 1, no. 1 (2001): 37–57.

Hendrix, Harville. *Getting the Love You Want: A Guide for Couples.* New York: Henry Holt, 2001.

Hendrix, Harville, and Helen LaKelly Hunt. *Giving the Love That Heals: A Guide for Parents.* New York: Atria Books, 1997.

His Holiness the Dalai Lama. *The World of Tibetan Buddhism: An Overview of Its Philosophy and Practice.* Translated by Geshe Thupten Jinpa. Somerville, MA: Wisdom Publications, 1995

His Holiness the Dalai Lama and Howard Cutter. *The Art of Happiness: A Handbook for Living.* New York: Riverhead Books, 1998.

Johnson, Susan. *Hold Me Tight: Seven Conversations for a Lifetime of Love.* New York: Little, Brown, 2008.

Larson, J. "Understanding Stepfamilies." *American Demographics* 14 (1992): 360.

Luthar, Suniya S., and Edward Ziegler. "Vulnerability and Competence: A Review of Research on Resilience in Childhood." *American Journal of Orthopsychiatry* 61, no. 1(1991): 6–22.

Lyubomirsky, Sonja. *The How of Happiness: A Scientific Approach to Getting the Life You Want.* New York: Penguin Press, 2008.

"Making Stepfamilies Work." American Psychological Association. Accessed August 27, 2012. http://www.apa.org/helpcenter/stepfamily.aspx.

Martin, Teresa Castro, and Larry L. Bumpass. "Recent Trends in Marital Disruption." *Demography* 26, no. 1 (1989): 37–51.

Masten, Ann S., and J. Douglas Coatsworth. "The Development of Competence in Favorable and Unfavorable Environments: Lessons from Research on Successful Children." *American Psychologist* 53, no. 2 (1998): 205–20.

McTaggart, Lynne. *The Intention Experiment: Using Your Thoughts to Change Your Life and the World.* New York: Free Press, 2008.

Moore, Thomas. *Care of the Soul: A Guide for Cultivating Depth and Sacredness in Everyday Life.* New York: HarperCollins, 1994.

Myss, Caroline, and Norman C. Shealy. *The Creation of Health: The Emotional, Psychological, and Spiritual Responses That Promote Health and Healing.* New York: Random House, 1988.

Nelsen, Jane, Cheryl Erwin, and H. Stephen Glenn. *Positive Discipline for Blended Families: Nurturing Harmony, Respect, and Unity in Your New Stepfamily.* New York: Prima Publications, 1997.

Norton, Arthur J., and Louisa F. Miller. Marriage, Divorce, and Remarriage in the 1990s. *Current Population Reports,* Series 23-180. Washington, DC: US Government Printing Office, 1992.

Norwood, Perdita K. *The Enlightened Stepmother: Revolutionizing the Role.* New York: Avon, 1999.

O'Conner, Anne. *The Truth about Stepfamilies in America.* New York: Marlowe, 2003.

Palmer, Nancy, William D Palmer, and Kay Marshall Strom. *The Family Puzzle: Putting the Pieces Together.* New York: Pinon Press, 1996.

Papernow, Patricia L. *Becoming a Stepfamily: Patterns of Development in Remarried Families.* San Francisco: Jossey-Bass, 1993.

Peterson, Christopher, and Martin E. P. Seligman. *Character Strengths and Virtues: A Handbook and Classification.* New York: Oxford University Press and Washington, DC: American Psychological Association, 2004.

Reivich, Karen, and Andrew Shatté. *The Resilience Factor: 7 Keys to Finding Your Inner Strength and Overcoming Life's Hurdles.* New York: Broadway Books, 2002.

———. *The Resilience Factor: 7 Essential Skills for Overcoming Life's Inevitable Obstacles.* New York: Broadway Books, 2002.

Ricard, Matthieu, and Daniel Goleman. *Happiness: A Guide to Developing Life's Most Important Skill.* New York: Little, Brown, 2003.

Riera, Michael. *Uncommon Sense for Parents with Teenagers.* Berkeley: Celestial Arts, 1995.

Bibliography

Rosenberg, Marshall B. *Nonviolent Communication: A Language of Life*. Encinitas, CA: PuddleDancer Press, 2003.

Schwartz, Jeffrey, and Sharon Begley. *The Mind & The Brain: Neuroplasticity and the Power of Mental Force*. New York: ReganBooks, 2002.

Seligman, Martin E. P. *Authentic Happiness: Using the New Positive Psychology to Realize Your Potential for Lasting Fulfillment*. New York: Free Press, 2003.

—————. *Learned Optimism: How to Change Your Mind and Your Life*. New York: Pocket Books, 1998.

—————. *The Optimistic Child: A Proven Program to Safeguard Children against Depression and Build Lifelong Resilience*. New York: Harper Perennial, 1995.

Seligman, Martin E. P., Tracy A. Steen, Nansook Park, and Christopher Peterson. "Positive Psychology Progress: Empirical Validation of Interventions." *American Psychologist* 60, no. 5 (2005): 410–42. doi:10.1037/0003-066X.60.5.410.

Siegel, Daniel J. *Mindsight: The New Science of Personal Transformation*. New York: Bantam, 2010.

Smith, Tom W. "The Emerging 21st Century Family." *GSS Social Change Report* No. 42. Chicago: University of Illinois National Opinion Research Center, 1999. Accessed August 27, 2012. http://publicdata.norc.org:41000/gss/DOCUMENTS/REPORTS/Social_Change_Reports/SC42.pdf.

"Stepfamily Statistics." Stepfamily Foundation. Accessed June 17, 2003. http://www.stepfamily.org/statistics.html.

Tolle, Eckhart. *A New Earth: Awakening to Your Life's Purpose*. New York: Penguin Group, 2006.

Werner, Emmy E. "Risk, Resilience, and Recovery: Perspectives from the Kauai Longitudinal Study." *Developmental Psychopathology* 5, no. 4 (1993), 503–15.

Werner, Emmy E., and Ruth S. Smith. *Journeys from Childhood to Midlife: Risk, Resilience, and Recovery*. Ithaca, New York: Cornell University Press, 2001.

Zukav, Gary. *Soul Stories*. New York: Fireside, 2000.

Made in the USA
San Bernardino, CA
29 February 2020